.The
Resistance

The Resistance

Gemma Malley

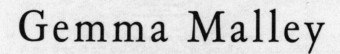

BLOOMSBURY

LONDON BERLIN NEW YORK SYDNEY

Bloomsbury Publishing, London, Berlin and New York

First published in Great Britain in 2008 by Bloomsbury Publishing Plc
36 Soho Square, London, W1D 3QY

This paperback edition first published 2009

A CIP catalogue record of this book is available from the British Library

ISBN 978 0 7475 8772 9

FSC
Mixed Sources
Product group from well-managed
forests and other controlled sources
Cert no. SGS - COC - 2061
www.fsc.org
© 1996 Forest Stewardship Council

Typeset by Dorchester Typesetting Group Ltd
Printed in Great Britain by Clays Ltd, St Ives Plc, Bungay, Suffolk

5 7 9 10 8 6 4

www.bloomsbury.com

For Mark, for always

Chapter One

Overhead lighting, bleak and uncompromising, shone down into the small room like a prison guard's searchlight, picking out every speck of dust, every mark on the cheap carpet, every smudged fingerprint on the window sill. It was a room which, Peter suspected, had been used for many purposes; the ghosts of its former occupants clung to it like cobwebs.

'Tell me how Peter is. Tell me what he's been thinking about lately.'

Peter looked into the eyes of the woman sitting in front of him and sat back in his chair, circling the gold ring around his finger. The ring had been the only thing he'd had with him when he was found as a baby.

The chair was padded, obviously intended to put him at ease, but it wasn't working. He rarely felt comfortable. Anna said it was because he liked to make things difficult for himself, but he wasn't sure. He figured that it just wasn't in his nature to feel too comfortable. Comfort made you lazy. It was the easy option.

'He's been thinking,' he said, smirking to himself as he adopted his counsellor's use of the third person, 'that his life sucks. That it's monotonous and boring and that there is very little point to him.'

His assimilation counsellor frowned; Peter felt adrenaline zip through his body. She was taken in. She looked concerned. It was a rare display of emotion – her face hardly ever expressed anything other than passive interest, however much he'd tried over the past few months. He studied her face. Her skin gave the initial impression of a light tan, but under the harsh overhead light you could see that actually it was covered in bronzing powder, little particles of orangey-brown dust nestling into the ridges around her eyes, around her mouth. She wore turquoise – a jacket and matching skirt. Her neck sagged. But Peter's eyes were drawn to her hair, which somehow didn't work. It was brown, with strands of blonde in it. At least, the hairs *looked* brown and blonde; they were white really, coloured regularly, religiously. Any sign of old age had to be eradicated. It was pathetic, he thought. Appearances were all that counted to people who took Longevity, not what lay beneath.

'Very little point to you? Peter, what do you mean by that?'

Peter rolled his eyes, feigning boredom. 'I mean that, before, I felt like I had a purpose. I knew what I was doing, knew why I was doing it. And now . . .' He trailed off, leaving the sentence hanging in mid-air.

'And now?' his counsellor prompted.

'And now I work in a small laboratory doing meaningless work, I live in a house I loathe, and I barely earn enough money to heat it, let alone buy books for Anna or food for Ben. I got her out of Grange Hall to be free, to enjoy life, and now . . . now I feel like it was all for nothing. I thought I was going to do something with my life, achieve something. But everything . . . it feels like everything was for nothing.'

His counsellor nodded thoughtfully. 'You feel that you're letting Anna down?' she asked.

Peter sighed; even in this contrived conversation he found the idea of letting Anna down hard to contemplate, even though he knew it wasn't true, would never be true.

'Maybe,' he said, shrugging.

'I'm sure she doesn't feel that way. Anna is a very sensible girl. She understands how the world works, Peter.'

Peter raised an eyebrow. Anna had seen her assimilation counsellor for just a few weeks; had been discharged from the programme early. So practised was she at gaining the trust of authority figures that she had managed to convince her counsellor in no time at all that she was no threat, that she would make a good, diligent citizen. It was something that Peter admired and resented in equal measure – she was only good at it because she'd had to be to survive at Grange Hall. Peter, on the other hand, had been unable to resist the odd caustic comment, the odd misplaced joke; several months later, he was still having to come every week to convince his counsellor that he could 'fit in' to society.

Peter crossed his arms and adopted a different look. A look that would tell her he was lost, that he was weak, that the Authorities had successfully crushed his spirit.

'I just want to provide for her,' he said, forcing himself not to smile at the look of understanding that crossed the counsellor's face.

'It's money that you're worried about?'

'Money, boredom . . .' He sat forward in his chair, placing his chin in his hands.

'And?' She was looking back at him now. 'Peter, you know that our discussions are completely confidential. What is said in this room stays in this room, I can assure you.'

Peter looked at her for a few seconds. He was almost impressed that she could tell such a blatant lie with such warmth in her voice. Maybe he'd underestimated her. 'I've begun to think seriously about my grandfather's offer,' he said in a low, soft voice.

Surprise flickered across her face just briefly, just enough for him to see.

'I see.' She paused. 'I thought you said that you would never have anything to do with him? That anyone who was involved in Longevity production was no relation of yours?'

Her eyes were twinkling slightly; she was playing with him. It was fair enough – he *had* said that. Many times. He'd meant it too.

'I know.' He dropped his eyes down and allowed his left hand to move over his right, let his fingers trace the flower engraved on his ring, the flower which he believed had drawn him to Anna, had fixed his destiny. It mustn't look as though he was taking this decision lightly. He had to make her think he was conflicted.

'I'm only thinking about it. I just . . .' Peter raised his eyes to meet hers slowly, and didn't look away. 'I just want more. There has to be more, you know? I mean, Anna, she reads books, she writes, she looks after Ben. Me – I've got nothing. Maybe if I worked for my grandfather, maybe if I made some money, maybe . . .'

'Maybe you'd find some meaning?'

'Yeah.'

Peter stood up and walked towards the window. It was covered by a grey, institutional blind that reminded him of Grange Hall. He pushed it aside and looked out at the streets below, which were equally grey. He couldn't see it, but he knew that somewhere in the distance the outline of Pincent Pharma would be dominating the skyline. 'Anyway,' he said, not turning around, 'I figure he owes me.'

'He owes you?'

Peter nodded and returned to his chair. 'He makes Longevity drugs, right?' he said, narrowing his eyes slightly. 'Well, Longevity drugs led to me being a Surplus. They're the reason I've spent most of my life being hidden and passed around. Which makes my grandfather the reason I had no childhood to speak of. He *owes* me.'

'You still seem angry, Peter.' His counsellor's voice was soft, controlled; she was doing her best to reassure him, but it had the opposite effect. He wondered if she spoke like that at home, off duty, wondered what she sounded like when she was angry or frustrated.

'I was angry,' he said, making his voice catch slightly – a brilliant touch that he would tell Anna about later. 'Really angry. But now . . . Now I'm not. Now . . .'

'Now you're wondering what to do with the rest of your life?'

Peter shrugged. 'I suppose,' he said. 'It's not like I've got many other options. I go for jobs and people look at me like I'm a freak. And I am a freak to them – I'm about a hundred years younger than most of them. At Pincent Pharma I could earn good money. My grandfather said the door was always open. So I thought I'd see if he meant it.'

'I'm sure he did,' his counsellor said. She looked relieved, like she thought she'd 'broken through'. He'd heard her once on the phone before an appointment when she was unaware that he was just outside the door. She'd told someone that she had yet to break through to him, that she was going to try a different tack. He'd been pleased – had seen it as a badge of honour that he was impenetrable, that he was difficult. 'I think it's a good idea, actually,' she continued, now making some notes. 'So how were you planning to tell him?'

The corners of Peter's mouth edged upwards involuntarily; immediately, he suppressed his smile. 'I already have,' he said quietly. 'I wrote him a letter. He left a message yesterday. Said I should start on Monday.'

His counsellor looked up at him with a start, then turned an impassive smile on him. 'I see,' she said thoughtfully. 'Well, let's see how it goes, shall we?'

Half an hour later, Peter left the Authorities building on Cheapside, and turned left down towards Holborn. The streets were fairly empty – which Peter considered a plus. In the well-ordered pedestrian zone there was only a trickle of shoppers and one or two people walking their dogs or power-walking themselves. Keeping his head down, he shoved his hands firmly in his pockets, a reflex from his days as a Surplus, from his days of hiding, from never knowing who might call the Catchers, never knowing what tomorrow might bring. The few people around narrowed their eyes as he passed, stared at him uncertainly, a mixture of envy and mistrust colouring their cheeks.

As he walked, he saw the usual posters on the sides of buildings, spread across billboards, advertising miracle creams, promoting exercise classes and education courses, cautioning people to conserve energy.

Others warned of population overload, urging people to watch out for 'illegal immigrants, Surpluses and other drains on our precious resources'. Like the Legals weren't the biggest drains of all.

He used to challenge posters like that all the time, used to plunge head first into arguments with anyone who'd listen, anyone who'd take him on, but now he'd learnt to keep his mouth shut. Not because he didn't want to fight any more, but because Pip had suggested that arguing for the sake of it wouldn't achieve much, that drawing attention to himself could do more damage than good – which Peter could sort of see, but it still frustrated him when he let things go, when he didn't fight people more.

Still, he told himself regularly, they'd see eventually. When the Underground triumphed, they'd all see. Cheered by this thought, Peter jumped on a tram heading for Oxford Street. As it reached Tottenham Court Road, he slipped off, then walked quickly down towards Cambridge Circus, turning right into Old Compton Street. From there he continued west into the underbelly of Soho, where small, darkened shops furtively sold their illicit wares – baby clothes, illegal drugs, disallowed foods, black market energy vouchers.

He looked at his watch – he was ten minutes early, but that was better than being late. Looking around cautiously, he entered an empty shop, walked past the builders who were busy refitting the place, down the stairs, and out through the back. From there, he walked down a narrow, dirty pathway towards a shabby wooden door and knocked quietly, four times.

Moments later, he sensed movement behind the door and it opened very slightly to reveal a man with a beard and a mop of untamed hair. He looked like a vagrant, and looked Peter up and down suspiciously.

'Cold for this time of year, isn't it?' he said gruffly.

'I find that exercise warms me up,' Peter replied. The man hesitated for a few moments, then pulled the door open, quickly bustling him in. The usual thrill Peter got from being part of something so covert, so important, darted through him like an electrical current. He didn't recognise the man on the door; he rarely saw the same guard twice. In fact, when he visited the Underground's headquarters he always found himself thinking he knew very little about the other members or how it was run. He was given directions and he followed them; his questions were met with wry smiles, evasive propaganda, or blank stares. It was for his protection, Pip told him. For everyone's protection.

'I'm here to see Pip,' Peter said, feeling himself straighten up, as if to impose himself more on his surroundings, which were familiar, yet alien. Every six months or so, the Underground's headquarters moved, leaving no trace of its activities. Peter had been to this building twice before, and each time it felt different, as if walls and doors had been moved around. What remained constant was the smell. The places the

Underground chose were always dirty, messy, half-derelict, easy to abandon.

To the left of the entrance were some stairs going down. A woman was coming up them, clutching her left arm. As she passed by Peter to get to the door, their eyes met with a flicker of recognition. Peter didn't know the woman, but he knew why she was here, knew that the top of her left arm would be bloody and painful where her contraceptive implant had been wrenched out by one of the Underground's doctors, knew that she was embarking on one of the most dangerous activities any human could take part in: the quest to become pregnant, to create new life.

The woman slipped out and Peter looked at the guard on the door, who said nothing, but motioned along the corridor behind him. At the end was a small room with a dim light.

Pip was waiting for him, sitting at a low table, his tall athletic frame hunched over it uncomfortably as if deep in thought. The founding father of the Underground, Pip was, to Peter, the nearest thing he'd known to a father – closer to him even than Anna's father had been. Pip had been there from the beginning, guiding him, helping him. Later, Peter had discovered that he wasn't the only one. Pip guided and led everyone in the Underground; everyone was equally in thrall to his hypnotic eyes, his unspoken power. Pip wasn't the Underground's official leader; it didn't have one, because Pip refused to let the structures and hierarchies of the hated Authorities infiltrate his 'group'. But he was the leader really; everyone deferred to his judgement and no decision was made without consulting him. He'd begun the fight against Longevity years ago all on his own, Mr Covey, Anna's father, had told Peter, writing leaflets, helping the parents of Surpluses, gradually attracting supporters until the Underground stretched the length and breadth of the country. Now the Underground had a massive network of similar groups abroad and had become so powerful that the Authorities had set up a dedicated department to fight them. All because of Pip.

But Pip would never talk about it. He didn't look much like a powerful leader either. He didn't seem to pay much attention to his appearance; his hair changed regularly to ensure he could blend in, to make sure he wasn't noticed, wasn't captured, but most of the time it was pretty unkempt. And he always insisted on meeting in shabby, run-down places – like this one: plain walls covered with peeling paint, a window greased to prevent anyone from seeing in, a solitary bulb doing its best to provide enough light, a table that wobbled every time he leant on it.

The Authorities had put a high price on Pip's head, published his picture on every street corner, on every news feed. But they still hadn't caught him. People said he was far too clever, that he was too well protected, but Peter suspected it was more than that. It was just the way Pip was. You wanted to help him.

You wanted him to like you, to respect you. Quite simply, he made you want to do everything you could to please him; it was why the Underground had never suffered from internal feuding, why people were joining all the time. Legend had it that a Catcher once discovered Pip in a disused warehouse, that hours later, instead of capturing him and claiming his reward, the Catcher was swearing allegiance to the Underground, that he was now one of its most valued soldiers. It didn't surprise Peter in the slightest.

'Good to see you, Peter,' Pip said softly, without looking up.

Peter smiled, immediately relaxing. 'Yeah, you too.'

Pip motioned for him to sit down, offered him a drink of water, then looked at Peter seriously. 'Things are getting more dangerous,' he said in a low voice. 'We carried out an attack on a couple of Longevity shipments recently and the Authorities are upping surveillance. We're going to have to be careful.'

'I'm always careful,' Peter said, a hint of defensiveness in his voice.

'I know you are. I mean all of us. The whole movement. There are spies everywhere.' He looked up briefly, and Peter was struck as always by his eyes, whirlpools of dark blue water that drew you in, inspired trust, made you want to do anything to make them shine with pride.

'You can count on me,' he said quietly.

'You're still starting on Monday?'

'Yes.' Peter nodded for added emphasis.

'And your counsellor?' The counsellor had worried Pip initially. He saw her as an agent of the Authorities, there to spy on Peter and wheedle information out of him; he worried about every word Peter uttered in her company. Until now, that was. Now she'd become a tool, a communication device.

'I told her I'm bored and frustrated and that I want more money,' Peter said, a note of pride in his voice.

'She didn't suspect anything?'

Peter grinned. 'Of course not. Anyway, I *am* bored and frustrated.' He raised an eyebrow at Pip, but Pip didn't smile; instead, he regarded Peter cautiously.

'Peter, are you sure you want to do this? Really sure?'

Peter rolled his eyes. 'Yes, I'm sure.'

'But you say you're frustrated?'

Peter sighed. He'd learnt long ago that Pip absorbed and analysed every word and gesture, intuited every emotion. Peter knew that this was how Pip held sway over people, but it was still annoying sometimes. 'Frustrated because the Authorities moved us to a hideous box house in the suburbs. Frustrated because they watch our every move and I still haven't taken Anna to the countryside because I can't get a permit to travel. Frustrated because there're old people everywhere and they stare at us like we don't belong here. That's all. I won't let it get in the way. I promise.'

Pip regarded Peter thoughtfully, then he stood up

and walked calmly around to the back of his chair. 'You mustn't let your emotions get the better of you. There is a great deal to be angry about, but anger doesn't change things.'

'I know. Action changes things.'

'Action, but also strength of will, Peter.'

Peter nodded seriously. 'I know. I'm strong, Pip. Come on, I've proved that, haven't I?'

'Of course you have,' Pip said, his voice warmer suddenly. 'Peter, you have proved yourself a thousand times. But you're going to be on your own, with the whole weight of Pincent Pharma's machine against you, and I need to know that you're prepared. You must realise that this isn't just a job, Peter. It's a battle. A battle of nature and science, good and evil. People get seduced by Longevity, and your grandfather will do everything in his power to win you over. You have to go into this with your eyes open.'

'My eyes *are* open,' Peter said, his eyes shining. 'I hate Richard Pincent. I hate everything he stands for. Longevity is responsible for everything bad in my life. Anna's life, too. I want to destroy it as much as you do.'

'I know you do.' Pip sat down again, and his eyes softened. 'And how is Anna? Is she OK with what you're doing?'

At the mention of Anna's name, Peter felt a warm glow surround him. 'She's fine. And she's as keen as I am to fight Longevity. You know that.'

'Of course I do,' Pip smiled. 'Well then, on Monday

morning you will report at Pincent Pharma as your grandfather requested.'

'As Richard Pincent told me,' Peter interrupted, his voice low.

'As Richard Pincent told you,' Pip corrected himself.

'And then what do I do?' Peter asked excitedly. 'Do I blow it up? Do I smash the machinery?'

Pip raised an eyebrow, his eyes twinkling. 'You keep a low profile and you take note of everything. And you learn, Peter.'

'That's it?' Peter's face fell slightly.

'That's a great deal,' Pip said. Then he leant closer. 'Peter, we have people in many places – in every Authorities department, in Longevity distribution companies, in prisons. But we've never had anyone at the heart of Pincent Pharma. No one with access to the information we need. Your eyes and ears are going to be your tools, Peter. Through you we can get to God himself.'

'God doesn't exist,' Peter said in a low voice. 'Everyone knows that.'

'No, he doesn't,' Pip agreed. 'But your grandfather is doing his best to become the most fearsome deity that the world has ever known. A deity that feeds on nothing but power and greed. A deity that must be stopped, for all our sakes.'

'So I just look and learn,' Peter said. 'OK. But is there anything I'm looking for? Anything specific? Do you need the formula of the drugs?'

'So we can make more?' Pip smiled and Peter felt himself go red. Pip's face turned more serious. 'I'm sorry, Peter, I shouldn't have laughed. It was a good question. So no, it isn't the formula we want. We want to . . .' His voice trailed off, as though he didn't want to finish the sentence.

'Want to what?' Peter demanded.

'The source of some of the new drugs coming out of Pincent Pharma,' Pip said thoughtfully. 'We're not sure what it is. We have our suspicions, but . . .'

'But what?'

Pip sighed. 'Peter, something tells me there're things going on inside the walls of Pincent Pharma, bad things behind the clean, professional facade. But whatever they are, they're well hidden.'

'What sort of bad things?' Peter asked.

'That,' Pip said, smiling again, 'is what you'll need to find out.' He stood up suddenly, his muscles tautening visibly as he moved. 'I'll be in touch, Peter.'

Peter nodded, stood up and turned to leave. Then he stopped. 'We are going to do it, aren't we?' he said softly. 'We are going to win?'

Pip put his hand on Peter's shoulder. 'Eventually, Peter. But I imagine there will be a few battles first.'

Peter looked up at him for a few seconds, then took a deep breath. 'You can count on me, Pip. I'll find out what's going on.'

'Good,' Pip said, his voice matter-of-fact now. He pulled out a file and handed it to Peter. 'Take this. Read it. Absorb it. Then get rid of it. And Peter?'

'What?'

'Good luck. Take care. And take care of Anna and Ben, won't you?'

'Of course.'

Peter left the room, making his way back along the corridor, past the gruff guard, through the passageway to the shop, then out into the road. He walked back along Old Compton Street, down towards Piccadilly, then jumped on a tram heading north towards Tottenham Court Road and, after that, another one heading south again. Eventually, he arrived at Waterloo Station to get his train home. Keep them guessing, he thought to himself. If the Authorities were watching him, and he was pretty sure they were, then he wanted at least to make their job more difficult.

He got off the train at Surbiton and looked around in disdain. A few months ago, he and Anna had been living in Bloomsbury, in the house that Anna's parents had lived happily in for years. It had been a lovely house – big and rambling, sunny and warm, a place as different from Grange Hall as it was possible to be. But soon after he and Anna became Legal, the letters started to arrive, then the official visitors, all saying the same thing: that the house was too big for them, that they would be better off in a 'more efficient space'. They'd resisted, at first – after all, the house was theirs, inherited from Anna's parents. But gradually, the visits had become more regular, the letters more threatening, until even Pip had shrugged sadly and told them that the move was probably inevitable, unless they wanted to antagonise the Authorities, that this fight was probably one that wasn't worth fighting. And so they had been moved to a box in the suburbs, where two shopping centres had replaced the high street, and the residents saw them as intruders.

Of course, the Authorities hadn't publicised his and Anna's escape to freedom; they didn't want people knowing that they'd outwitted the Catchers, that they'd got out of a Surplus Hall alive. Nor had the Authorities said much about the death of Anna's parents, or the murder of Peter's father. They'd done their best to brush the stories under the carpet, to lose them in a mass of red tape. But stories like that didn't die very easily. Word had got out, newspapers had printed photographs of him and Anna with headlines questioning the effectiveness of the Catchers, asking whether the 'Life for a Life' policy should be revisited. No one wanted any additional burdens on the world's meagre resources and that was all he and Anna represented to most people. So neighbours avoided them, shop assistants regarded them warily and passers-by either stared at them curiously or pretended they didn't exist. Not that Peter cared. He knew he had as much right to be there as anyone else. More right.

Thrusting his hands in his pockets, he walked through the Amenities Park, where various outdoors exercise classes seemed to take place at every hour of the day. There were people running, jogging, touching their toes, stretching their muscles – a grand exhibition of strength, of energy, of life. Or, rather, fear of dying, Peter thought cynically.

It wasn't just death that people feared, either; it was ageing, decay. Legs and arms could be replaced; key organs could be regrown. But those little lines around the mouth, that lethargy in the morning that started to last all day, the feeling of having seen it all before – these were things that had to be fought. Peter had read all about it in *The New Times* and the lifestyle supplement of *Staying Young*, usually whilst waiting for appointments with his assimilation counsellor. The scientists had done their bit, the journalists would write; it was up to individuals to maximise the potential of Longevity – to live their lives to the full, to maintain a youthful energy and enthusiasm.

Or they could bow out gracefully and leave youth to the young, Peter thought. They could take a long hard look at themselves – at their endless, boring lives – and ask whether death might not be such a bad idea after all. People might think they had learnt to delay the inevitable, but underneath the veneer of Longevity, if they were honest about it, they would see that the rot had still set in. Like an apple that looks fresh but reveals maggots inside, people could not ignore for ever the fact that they were all past their sell-by date.

He turned on to his street, the ugly and monotonous row of identical houses. And yet, as he approached Number 16, he still felt the familiar feeling of a weight being lifted, a sense of a gap in the clouds that seemed to dog his every move. It was home. Not the bricks and mortar – the house was, in Peter's opinion, a monstrosity, a soulless building with small, oppressive rooms and low ceilings; but what lived within it meant everything to him. As he approached the house, he could see Anna through the window, sitting on the sofa reading, knees bent under her.

Before his key had entered the lock, he heard her jump up and come running to the door. She pulled it open and smiled up at him.

'You're home!' The smile was short-lived; immediately it was replaced by a frown. 'And you're late. You said you'd be home an hour ago.'

'Yeah, sorry about that . . .' His eyes were shining, but he kept his voice low out of habit; the Underground had swept the house for bugs but Pip had admitted that they couldn't be a hundred per cent sure the house was secure. 'Is Ben asleep?'

He kissed Anna gently on her nose, which she wrinkled.

'Dead to the world,' she confirmed. 'So?'

Peter walked into the sitting room, flopping down on the same sofa Anna had been on just a few moments before. He could feel her warmth on the cushions. Before he'd met Anna, he'd thought he'd known what love was, thought he'd understood about friendship, romance, all of it, but he hadn't – not at all. Until he'd held Anna in his arms, until he'd let her see his soul, until he'd heard her cry gently when he made love to her for the first time, he'd known nothing. And now, sometimes, when it was just the two of them, when he smelt her hair, caught her eye, he felt as though he knew all there was to know about everything, as though they knew the secret of life. A secret far more powerful than Longevity, far more long-lasting.

'So what?' he teased.

Anna pretended to punch him. 'How did it go?' she mouthed silently, taking his hand, her eyes alert.

'It was fine,' he whispered. Then, winking, he pulled himself off the sofa, wandered into the kitchen and flicked on the kettle. An electronic voice immediately piped up: 'How much hot water do you really need? Remember, less water, less waste.'

'Fine?' Anna whispered, following him. 'What does that mean? You are so annoying sometimes.'

'Me or the kettle?'

'You're both as bad as each other,' Anna replied out loud, raising her eyebrows.

Peter grabbed her, pulled her in towards him and kissed her. 'It was fine,' he murmured in her ear. 'She bought the story, hook, line and sinker. And then I saw Pip and everything's set.'

Anna smiled, her expression at once excited and apprehensive. Then she pulled away, took out two mugs and put tea bags in them. 'So you must be looking forward to starting at Pincent Pharma on Monday,' she said out loud. She was still smiling, but

Peter could see a hint of tension in her eyes, of worry.

'Certainly am,' he confirmed. Then he grabbed her again, this time more playfully. 'And by Tuesday, I'll have been fired and I'll have to get a job as an aerobics instructor,' he whispered.

'No, you won't! You can't. You've got to destroy it, Peter, you've got to,' Anna whispered back, pulling away and looking at him wide-eyed, evidently not entirely sure whether he was joking or not. Which was perfectly understandable; Peter wasn't sure either.

Chapter Two

Pincent Pharma occupied a prime position in south-west London, on the river. The building had existed for years in various guises – as a power plant, as an art gallery – before Pincent Pharma Inc convinced the town planners and the Authorities that Longevity drugs required a London production centre. Within months, building work had begun and soon the large, dark landmark had been transformed into a huge white church of Longevity. Inside its walls, hundreds of the best minds were devoted to researching, creating, producing, improving and preaching the benefits of the small white pills that had enabled humans to achieve the ultimate goal – never-ending life.

Peter knew nothing about architecture, but he could feel the building's power, its arrogance, its secrecy, as he walked around its boundaries. He was shivering, and not just because of the cold winter wind that froze his face. This was the place where Longevity drugs were made. This was the place he despised, that he'd always despised. And today he was going inside.

The building gave little away from the outside. Painted white, with Pincent Pharma emblazoned across its gates, the laboratory had small windows with mirrored glass, ensuring that anyone peering in to spy on the workings of the employees within would be met only by a reflection of their own squinting eyes and curious expression. Around the building was a high wall, impenetrable except for several large gates, one of which allowed pedestrians through and either side of which was stationed a security guard in a toughened glass and steel booth, along with an identi-card scanner which automatically opened and closed the gate.

Foreign terrorists fighting for cheap Longevity drugs in their own countries had tried several times to bomb Pincent Pharma; the laboratory was, though, apparently indestructible. Bomb-proof, fire-proof, flood-proof, damage-proof – he'd read about it in the file Pip had given him. Longevity production was considered more important even than farming, which itself was a high priority for the Authorities. *Comfort, Health, Wealth and Learning* were the stated aims of the Authorities – these things were what mattered to people, what resonated with them. The only thing that mattered was to keep everyone alive and happy. What didn't matter was people like him and Anna. New people. New life. Like Noah's Ark, the Authorities had pulled up the gangplank many years before and set sail defiantly, not caring what they might be leaving behind, or to what horrific world they might be sailing.

And now, he was going to be working inside this place. Peter, who had approached the building from its back in order to size it up before formally presenting himself to Richard Pincent, suppressed a slight shudder at the thought as he walked around the perimeter wall. Along it, posters gleamed in new glass casings, the Pincent Pharma logo clearly visible across the top of each of them, navy on white, the final 'a' in Pharma given a little tail that suggested a friendly smile.

As he approached the gate, Peter steeled himself. Steadily, he walked towards it.

The guard appeared not to see him, looked past him, as though his existence was of no importance at all.

'I'm Peter,' Peter said, looking him right in the eye. 'Peter . . .'

'Peter Pincent?' the guard asked lazily. He was thin, wiry; a scar just above his left eye suggested that he had seen action.

Peter frowned. He hated his surname. Loathed it.

He nodded.

The security guard looked him up and down, unaware that Peter was also scrutinising him. The guard was about a hundred and forty, Peter guessed.

'You'll need to fill in a few forms,' the man said, handing Peter a clipboard then leaning against the wall of his booth. There was a little smirk on his lips, as though he was playing with Peter, as though he was party to some joke. Peter's eyes narrowed. He hated authority figures, people who thought that a uniform and a job title gave them the right to order people around, to order *him* around.

Irritated, Peter began to scrawl his name, address, date of birth and purpose of visit on the forms he'd been given; the guard appeared to enjoy his awkward attempts to lean on the flimsy board behind them.

'You were in one of those Surplus Halls, weren't you?' It was a statement as much as a question, a way to show Peter that he had no secrets.

Peter nodded tightly. 'That's right.'

The security guard's lips crept upwards into a sneer. 'Lucky, aren't you?' he said, not waiting for an answer. 'And now you're coming to make Longevity drugs. Interesting career move.'

Peter took a deep breath and handed the form back to the guard. 'Now, where should I go?'

The guard folded his arms and looked Peter up and down again. Then he shrugged.

'You don't have a security pass, do you? Can't go through without a security pass.'

'And where do I get a security pass?'

'Reception.'

'And I can't get to reception –'

'Without a security pass. It's a tricky one.' The guard's eyes glinted slightly. Peter gave him a sarcastic smile.

'So it looks like I'm going to be spending the day right here, then,' he said. 'Now, do you think I should sit on that patch of gravel just there, or over on the concrete?'

The guard didn't say anything for a few seconds. Then he opened the gate. 'You know,' he muttered, 'only the best get to work here. People have to pass exams, wait years for a vacancy. Not everyone can just waltz in. You might want to watch yourself in there.'

'I absolutely will,' Peter said drily. 'And thanks for the compliment.'

'For what?'

'For saying I'm the best,' he said lightly. 'I am working here, after all.'

'You want to be careful,' the guard said, his voice suddenly taking on a menacing tone. 'Because I'll be watching you. I'll be watching you like a hawk.' He set off through the gates, motioning Peter to follow him, and walked towards the imposing doors at the front of the building.

The sky was still dark outside, but Jude was restless, couldn't sleep. Sighing, he pulled himself out from underneath his bedcovers and pulled on some trousers, two jumpers and a coat. He navigated the small patch of bare carpet in his bedroom that enabled him to get to the door, then went downstairs, swearing at the cold beneath his feet. Silently he made himself some coffee, then returned upstairs to take up his usual position at his computer. He stared at it moodily. He didn't feel like doing any work, would rather be trying out a new computer game he'd found, a relic from the twenty-first century that he was planning to adapt to a new platform, but he needed money. There was no food in the kitchen in spite of increasingly agitated reminders from his fridge to place an order, and he was going to run out of energy in twenty-four hours if he didn't top it up soon.

With a sigh, he pulled up his latest project and lazily started to type. His work was sporadic but well paid; whenever funds became low, he would hack into the systems of a bank or major institution that relied on technology for its survival, then call them up and offer to improve their firewalls, for a price. It was easy money – he had a reputation now and occasionally work even came to him.

An hour later, and money banked, he checked his watch, then, taking a gulp of the coffee he'd made earlier and which was now horribly cold, brought back up his spycode programme. He had developed it himself and updated it every couple of months; now at Version 16 it was able to render any system powerless. Most systems, anyway.

His first computer had been a gift from his father ten years ago when Jude had been six. 'Something to keep you occupied,' his father had said, his breath infused with alcohol. 'See if you can teach yourself to use it.' It had been an Authorities computer, declassified during the Electronic Shutdown, when the Authorities led organisations everywhere in lessening their energy footprint. Smaller, more efficient machines were introduced – functional computers that offered word-processing, messaging, no colour, no downloads. But Jude's was old school, a relic by most standards. Its functionality wasn't great – but it allowed him to do what he wanted. On it, he'd discovered something he was good at, better than anyone else he'd ever come up against. He'd written codes, programmes that were far more advanced than anything the Authorities had thought of themselves. He'd even tried to show his father – had thought that he would be interested, impressed. But the Director General of the Interiors Ministry hadn't been interested; had said he was too busy, had seemed embarrassed by his son's attentions. It hadn't taken Jude long to realise that the computer hadn't been a gift but a sop. Not that he was bothered. He didn't need his father to care about him; he didn't need anyone.

He navigated carefully, delicately breaking through several firewalls, guessing and second-guessing file names and locations. And then, across his screen, the view from a CCTV monitor flashed into life; his eyes widened slightly with excitement when he realised he'd timed it to perfection. He'd know that figure anywhere – that walk, shifty and arrogant at the same time. Jude had seen Peter on news programmes, in the newspapers; he'd even seen him on the street once. But this was much better. This was real.

'How the mighty revolutionary has fallen,' Jude

muttered to himself as he zoomed in, focused on Peter's face, his impenetrable expression. He didn't look much like someone who could break out of a Surplus Hall and evade capture by the Catchers. Didn't look like someone who had supposedly been working for the Underground since he was a baby. But these were the stories that circulated. Peter Pincent. The name had haunted Jude ever since he'd discovered who he was; his very presence made Jude's life both precious and guilt-ridden. Jude had been the lucky one, he knew that, had been told enough times; he was the one who was Legal. But now Peter was too. Now they were almost on a level pegging.

Jude clicked on the camera facing Pincent Pharma's main entrance, enhanced the zoom slightly, and followed Peter all the way to the perimeter gates. He slumped back in his chair and watched as Peter approached the security guard; a few minutes later, the two of them walked up towards the gates which opened, then closed behind them like a whale swallowing fish. Feeling his curiosity grow, Jude pulled the coat that doubled as a dressing gown tighter against the cold – all his energy coupons went towards his computer, not central heating or clothes.

Picking up, and then rejecting, his coffee cup, he found his eyes drawn back to the Pincent Pharma camera system. It was a sophisticated set-up, with almost impenetrable codes protecting it. But 'almost' hadn't protected it from Jude.

Idly, he pressed the tab key on his keyboard.

Immediately, he found himself looking at the back of Pincent Pharma, where a deserted path meandered down towards the river. He tabbed again – now he was looking at another path, surrounded by woodland, leading down to Battersea. Again, there was nothing to see. Except for the odd protest, which was always dissolved swiftly, the area surrounding Pincent Pharma tended to be fairly desolate. The nearest high street was a mile away; all habitable dwellings nearby had been demolished when Pincent Pharma had moved in – now all that was left was a kind of wasteland to the back and a patch of trees to the front. There was just one private road leading through the gates, connecting it to a perimeter road. At the back of the building, this perimeter road met a path down to the river; at the front, a slip road joined with the main road, along which armoured trucks could regularly be seen transporting Longevity drugs.

Jude tabbed through the cameras once more, just to see if there was anything worth looking at. He frowned. Something was different at the front. Something was wrong. Jude was very proud of his instinct for such things – he had spent years learning about economic theory and moral relativism from a series of expensive private tutors secured by his father, but Jude trusted his instinct over learning every time.

Staring at the screen in front of him, he could see clearly the outline of several men emerging from behind the trees. They were dressed in khaki – some kind of paramilitary uniform – and in their hands they clutched weapons of death: guns, rifles. Jude felt his heart quicken with excitement, though outwardly he remained still. Even to himself he liked to feign boredom and disinterest.

Silently, he watched as four armoured trucks swung into view, turning right into the slip road from the Pincent Pharma private road, the grey smoke from their engines disappearing into the cloudy sky. Jude flicked from camera to camera, watching as the trucks trundled further away from Pincent Pharma, picking up speed until they were turning out on to the main road, and then, suddenly, the truck at the front of the convoy swerved off to the right. A few seconds later it was followed by the second and third trucks; the fourth managed to brake before skidding to a halt across two lanes and crashing into the third.

Immediately, the khaki-dressed men emerged from the pathway and Jude realised that he had underestimated their numbers; it was a small army that swooped on the trucks, shooting their guns at the doors, pulling out the contents, pouring something on top of them before setting them alight. The drivers of the trucks didn't attempt to get out; instead, Jude could see them frantically speaking into their phones. Minutes later, more vehicles could be seen pulling out of Pincent Pharma's gates and speeding towards the trucks and the small, pungent fires on the road, but already, the men were disappearing – back up the pathway, along the road, behind walls. Jude watched, wide-eyed, his heart beating loudly in his chest. It had to be the Underground, he realised. He was finally seeing them in action.

Quickly Jude tabbed back to get a shot of the road, where men in Pincent Pharma security uniforms were helping the drivers out the trucks and attempting to put out the fires. He saw one of the security guards shout something, then, moments later, they were dragging two of the Underground men out from the path. The men were soon surrounded, their weapons wrestled from them.

One of the guards pulled out a walkie-talkie and said something into it. Two other guards immediately pulled the prisoners' hands behind their backs and handcuffed them.

Then a guard was shouting something and pointing his gun at one of the prisoners, and before Jude realised what was happening, the prisoner had fallen to his knees, blood pouring from his head. Jude caught his breath, recoiling backwards but unable to look away from the heap of khaki and the oozing red on the road. The man was dead. Actually dead. Jude's eyes flickered up to the other guards, who had stepped back, their expressions a mixture of horror and disgust.

The guard with the walkie-talkie barked something, then grabbed the remaining Underground prisoner whose eyes were fixed on his dead comrade, his face white. The prisoner was shouting something, trying to fight as they dragged him away, but it was useless.

Jude sat back on his chair, barely daring to breathe. For a long time, he sat like that, perfectly still. He'd seen a man die. In a world where death didn't occur it had shocked him to his core.

And then he shook himself. It was only real, after all. Reality wasn't as important as people made it out to be; to Jude it was simply the physical state in which he found himself, an environment he had limited control over. Pushing all thoughts of the Underground soldiers from his head, Jude exited the Pincent Pharma system and pulled up MyWorld, the virtual reality environment he'd been building, and surveyed his work. It was summer in MyWorld. The streets were thronged with people – young people; in its large parks, ageing adults were nowhere to be seen. Instead teenagers played football, shared jokes, sat around smoking and using mobile phones with no police harassing them. Grinning, Jude made his way along a short path to his usual spot, a bench, from where he could survey his dominion. Just as he knew she would be, his red-haired girlfriend was waiting for him smiling, looking hot in her short denim skirt.

'Hi, Jude2124,' she said, her voice sultry. 'I've missed you. Where've you been?'

Jude2124 grinned. 'It doesn't matter. The important thing is that I'm here now.'

*

Peter turned to see what was going on. He could hear a commotion on the main road, but it was several hundred metres away and the high walls prevented him from seeing anything. The guard turned and sneered at him.

'Jumpy, are we? Little bang got you scared?'

Peter didn't reply; he just shoved his hands in his pocket, then watched as the guard swiped a card, pressed his fingers against a glass pad, then allowed his eyes to be scanned. Finally, the heavy doors slid open to reveal a lobby, behind which four great escalators stretched upwards. A man walked towards Peter and the guard, a serious expression on his face. Peter felt himself stiffen; the man was Richard Pincent. The guard gave a brief salute.

'Peter,' Richard said, a brief smile appearing on his lips. 'Excuse me just one minute, won't you? Little disturbance outside.' He looked at the guard, the smile gone. 'You need to get back to your post. We've got a Code X.' The guard nodded, his face grim, then turned and walked quickly back towards the gate, pulling a walkie-talkie out of his pocket and clamping it to his ear.

Peter watched him leave, then turned back to his grandfather, who was barking orders into a small device that looked like a tiny phone; his voice was low and inaudible, but the tension could be felt. Then he put the phone in his pocket, looked back at Peter and smiled again.

'Come with me,' he said, then clapped his arm

around Peter's shoulder. 'Welcome to Pincent Pharma, Peter. Welcome to the most advanced laboratory in the whole world. The envy of scientists everywhere. Welcome to your new world.'

Chapter Three

The lobby was vast, larger than Peter had expected from the outside. This was a place that could devour you if you weren't careful, render you as insignificant as a flake of snow. As he followed his grandfather up one of the escalators, he tried his best not to be impressed by the scale of the place: walls that rose up a few hundred metres, huge screens displaying scientific diagrams, everything so white, so clean, so pure.

'Quite a sight, isn't it?' his grandfather said dramatically. 'This building's been here nearly a hundred years and I still catch my breath sometimes.'

Peter nodded, feigning enthusiasm, as his eyes darted around, looking for cameras, for anything important that Pip would find useful. He noted, archly, that there weren't any pictures of Surplus Halls anywhere, nothing proudly displaying the darker side of Longevity; when his grandfather caught his eye and held it for a few seconds, Peter found himself wondering if Pincent Pharma's surveillance system was so sophisticated that it could read his mind, but he knew that was impossible.

'This way.' They'd reached the top of the escalator and in front of them was a long corridor stretching to the right and left. His grandfather turned left and, after a few paces, turned right into another long corridor. 'Easy to get lost, if you don't know where you're going,' he said, leading Peter to a large viewing gallery that overlooked the reception atrium. Along it to the rear ran huge glass windows, through which rooms and laboratories were visible.

'Through here,' his grandfather said, walking briskly and pointing to his right, 'is the main production area. Of course, you can't see it. It's so well protected it doesn't have windows. What you can see is the finishing area where each tablet is pressed with the Pincent Pharma logo.'

Peter turned to see machine after machine whirring, white tablets pouring out of them in their thousands. Around the machines men and women stood monitoring operations, checking quality, their faces creased in concentration. One looked up and saw Richard; immediately he looked away and began to examine the machine next to him as though his life depended on it.

'Very important room that,' Richard said, walking on. 'The logo is how you know your drugs are genuine. Now, this area is one of our research labs.'

He led Peter to a large laboratory full of people in white coats staring into microscopes, into screens, into test tubes.

'What are they doing?' Peter asked.

Richard laughed. 'Working on improvements, of course. The world doesn't stand still, Peter. There's always something better.'

Peter nodded. 'And how do you know they work? I mean, who do you test the drugs on?'

He turned to look at his grandfather who stopped walking for a fraction of a second, then continued marching. 'We have extensive testing programmes,' he said dismissively. 'People will do anything for money, you know.'

'And you use stem cells, don't you?' Peter asked. 'Where do you get them? You must need so many!'

His grandfather stopped suddenly. 'You have a lot of questions,' he said.

Peter felt the hairs on the back of his neck stand up. Had he asked too much too soon? Did his grandfather suspect something? 'I want to learn,' he said.

Richard paused for a moment, then nodded. 'Yes, yes, of course you do. Well, I have the very thing. Follow me.'

Peter followed him, his eyes hungrily taking in every corridor, every door, every person they passed. Eventually, Richard opened a door and Peter followed him into a lecture theatre.

'A bit of history,' his grandfather said. 'We used to have quite a big educational programme here – students coming round, learning about Renewal and Longevity. That was back when we still had universities, of course. Now we use this room for ReTraining programmes,

Induction, foreign delegations, that sort of thing. We've got some educational packs, if you'd like one?'

The question, Peter realised immediately, was a rhetorical one; a pack was thrust into his hands and, under his grandfather's gaze, he felt compelled to open it. There were several pages of text outlining the history of Pincent Pharma, punctuated by boxes with trite information, which he scanned briefly.

Did you know?
- *It takes two weeks to produce each and every Longevity tablet*
- *Pincent Pharma employs over 5,000 of the world's best scientists, all dedicated to improving your quality of life*
- *For maximum benefits, your doctor should review your dosage every year*

Did you know?
- *Pincent Pharma supplies Longevity drugs to more than 100 countries worldwide*
- *Pincent Pharma developed the first ever Longevity drug in 2015 and still owns the worldwide patent*
- *Pincent Pharma quality checks every single Longevity tablet to exacting standards before they leave the production line*

Richard Pincent smiled benevolently. 'Now, you find yourself somewhere to sit down and we'll get started, shall we?'

Closing the pack, Peter made his way to a seat in the middle of the room. It was a small, push-down seat surrounded by a hundred or so others, all empty. As soon as he sat down, the theatre was plunged into darkness, and the screen at the front flickered into life.

On screen was Peter's grandfather, looking slightly younger, standing in a vast, open-plan laboratory, full of workstations at which serious-looking scientists in white coats were positioned.

'Welcome to Pincent Pharma, and the Institute of Cell Research. Under this roof, in these state-of-the-art facilities, thousands of scientists are researching the wonderful potential of cells. Cells that we at Pincent Pharma have adapted to cure human disease. Cells which we have reproduced in order to conquer degenerative conditions and catastrophic injuries. Cells which have now provided us with the ultimate answer to all the ills that have ever befallen mankind, scientific breakthroughs which have transformed not just medicine, not just science, but society at large. Welcome to the home of Longevity, the home of the future of mankind . . .'

Peter's on-screen grandfather walked towards the camera.

'What you are about to witness is no less than a miracle. A revolution. A change so huge that it dwarfs any other human achievements. What you are about to discover is the secret to eternal life.'

Rousing music started to play and Peter shifted

awkwardly in his seat. He turned round to see if his real grandfather was still in the room, but he couldn't see in the darkness.

He turned back to the screen to see a cartoon depicting several small, spherical blobs.

'The stem cell,' his grandfather's voice boomed. 'Such a small thing, and yet so powerful. Back in the twentieth century, scientists could only guess at the potential of these tiny cells. Cures for diseases that wiped out millions of lives every year. Helping the paralysed to regain movement in their limbs. Growing organs for transplantation. Scientists all over the world were racing to unlock the secrets of these tiny cells, to harness their capability.

'But one man went further. One man wanted more than simply to cure disease, to treat the sick. One man saw beyond the curative powers in cell therapy. One man saw that humankind's destiny was inexorably linked to the power of the stem cell. He knew, knew without any question, that the right combination, the right cells, used in the right way, could cure not just disease, but the most significant human condition of all. He knew that he could cure mortality.'

There was a brief pause and then the camera zoomed in on one of the blobs.

'So how did he do it? Well, it was with the help of these fellows. Meet the stem cell,' his grandfather's voice continued, now more jovial in tone. 'This clever creature can turn itself into any cell in the body. It could be a liver cell, a blood cell, a spinal cord cell. It can repair damage, replicate itself to replace ageing cells, prevent cancerous cells from developing.'

The blob developed a face and danced around the screen, fitting into various organs successfully, all the time grinning happily to itself.

Then the blob disappeared and his grandfather was on the screen again, this time outside a white pod with sliding doors, through which men in white coats could be seen walking. 'But whilst these cells have been known about since the twentieth century,' his grandfather was saying in an avuncular tone, 'only Pincent Pharma has leveraged their capability to create the most powerful drug known to man: Longevity.'

Peter's grandfather disappeared again and was replaced by a film of two old people walking along the street, bent over, their faces lined, their hair grey. Peter found himself wincing at the sight in spite of himself.

'Old age,' his grandfather's voice boomed. 'For thousands of years the unavoidable plight of humankind. Loss of key functions – hearing, eyesight, flexibility, strength. Loss of recall and brain capacity. A slow, painful degenerative process that ended more often than not in disease and then death. Eighty years was considered a good lifespan. At sixty, humans were considered too old to work, too old to contribute to society. But no longer.'

The shot switched to a film of some men playing a

game of football in the park. 'Where once humans had collapse, they now have Renewal. Where once humans accepted decay, they now enjoy an enhanced lifestyle. On that momentous day when natural scientist Dr Albert Fern discovered the true potential of stem cells, he changed the course of history.'

There was another pause, as Peter's on-screen grandfather surveyed the room, his eyes shining, then his face took on a slightly more humble expression as a new voice took over the story. 'Sadly, Dr Fern didn't live long enough to develop Renewal further, but Richard Pincent, his son-in-law and founder of Pincent Pharma, worked tirelessly after his death to extend the benefits of stem cells to people worldwide . . .'

Peter's eyes widened. So Albert Fern was Richard Pincent's father-in-law? That meant he was Peter's great-grandfather. He was related to the guy responsible for all of this. The thought made him shiver slightly.

The screen returned to Pincent Pharma, to the original open-plan laboratory shot. Peter's grandfather was now walking amongst the scientists, whilst the voice-over continued: '. . . ever since then, this noble company has been working for humanity to deliver Longevity, the drug that made history. That has *superseded* history. Scientists the world over have tried to replicate it, have tried to discover the formula, but to no avail. And now, Pincent Pharma's scientists continue to innovate, to deliver improvements to the formula; to discover even more ways to improve the quality of the human life. From tooth decay to limb regrowth, Pincent Pharma is at the forefront of human science, and we'll never stop looking for a better world for everyone.'

The camera panned back through several corridors, through the front doors until the entire building could be seen on screen, although not the white perimeter wall, the gates or the security guards.

'Pincent Pharma is science,' a voice said. 'Pincent Pharma is the future. Your future, and everyone on the planet's future. Thank you for taking the time to be with us. We hope that you enjoy your visit.'

The screen went black, then white words appeared: *Longevity and Renewal are the trademarks of Pincent Pharma Incorporated. Any attempt to copy, imitate or infringe intellectual copyright will result in prosecution.* The words gradually faded away until Peter found himself staring at a blank screen. And then the lights came on. Peter turned to see his grandfather was standing at the end of his row of seats.

'So, what did you think?'

Peter was thinking about his ring. His ring with 'AF' engraved on it.

'Very . . . interesting,' he said.

'Isn't it!' His grandfather's voice sounded excited, but his eyes suggested that he was distracted, thinking of something else. 'You know, Peter,' he said thoughtfully, 'there's so much for you to discover here.'

Peter smiled to himself. He hoped for Pip's sake

that he'd be able to discover it all.

'So tell me, Peter. Why, now, have you decided to take me up on my offer of work?'

The question came from nowhere and took Peter by surprise.

'I . . .' he started to say, calling up the speech he'd prepared just for this purpose. But his grandfather waved his hand to silence him.

'It's all right, I already know,' he said dismissively. 'At least I know what you wrote in your letter and I know what you told your counsellor. But we shouldn't always believe what we're told, should we, Peter?'

Peter looked at him uncertainly. 'No?'

'No.' His grandfather smiled. 'I like to keep an open mind. So let me say this one thing. I am confident that you will enjoy your time here, that you'll make the most of the opportunity you've been presented with. But step out of line, do anything that causes me any concern at all, and I can promise you, you'll wish that you hadn't.'

'OK,' Peter said. 'That's pretty clear.'

Richard laughed. 'Yes, Peter, it is.' Then his face turned serious. 'And there is one more thing.'

'Yes?' Peter asked.

'Longevity is here to stay, Peter. Everyone is here to stay. That's the way of the world now, and nothing is going to change that. Do you understand?'

Peter studied his grandfather's face for a few seconds, trying to decide on a response.

'Perfectly,' he said eventually, looking at his grandfather intently. 'And I don't intend to cause you any concern. I'm just pleased to have the opportunity to work here, that's all.'

Richard's eyes rested on him for a few seconds, then he nodded curtly.

'Good,' he said. 'That's very good.'

He motioned for Peter to follow him out of the lecture hall, and they walked in silence back down the corridor.

'I think it's time to introduce you to Dr Edwards, your teacher,' he said, when they reached a blue door. 'You won't find it hard – Pincents are born scientists . . .' He lifted his hand to push the door; as Peter followed him through it, he found himself in the same laboratory he'd seen in the film. Only now the workstations were all empty.

His grandfather noticed his frown and smiled. 'We built new facilities on the east side of the building,' he explained. 'Bigger and better. This is the ReTraining area now. You can learn and try things out to your heart's content. And this . . .' he pointed to a tall, slight man who was walking towards them quickly, 'is Dr Edwards, one of our most eminent scientists, and now the Head of ReTraining. For the next six months he will be your teacher and mentor, so I wouldn't get into his bad books.'

His grandfather's tone was silky, almost patronising, but Dr Edwards didn't seem to notice; he smiled modestly. 'Oh, I wouldn't worry about that, Peter,' he said warmly. 'It's very good to meet you. Very good indeed. Your grandfather has told me all about you.'

Peter looked at him carefully, building up a picture in his head. He took in the furrowed brow, the grey hair that Dr Edwards had evidently decided not to bother dyeing, his intelligent eyes, his open body language. He could pass for fifty, but Peter suspected that he was at least double that. He was clever, Peter surmised; introverted and passionate about his work.

'Hi,' Peter said. 'Good to meet you, too.'

'So, Peter, what's your science like? Are you an expert, or is your knowledge more . . . rudimentary, would you say?' Dr Edwards asked.

Peter raised an eyebrow. 'I'd say "rudimentary" just about covers it.'

'Good.' Dr Edwards nodded. 'When people know a lot, we have to spend a great deal of time getting them to unlearn it,' he explained. 'Most of what people have been taught is years out of date, hardly relevant at all. A clean slate is far easier.' His face was earnest, Peter decided, well meaning. If he weren't involved in Longevity drugs, Peter might even have liked him.

'Right, well, I'll leave you to it, then,' Richard Pincent said. 'Peter, concentrate, won't you? Dr Edwards has a great deal to teach you.'

Peter nodded silently, his eyes following his grandfather until the door had closed behind him.

'I'm sure you'll be a fast learner,' Dr Edwards smiled. 'After all, it's in your blood.'

'Oh, I'm not much like my grandfather,' Peter said lightly.

'Your grandfather?' Dr Edwards frowned. 'Oh, no. I was thinking more about your great-grandfather. Albert Fern. The greatest scientist who ever lived.'

Peter swallowed uncomfortably, then looked up at Dr Edwards, forcing an enthusiastic expression on to his face. 'So, where do I start?'

Chapter Four

Richard Pincent watched, hidden behind one-way glass, as the man was forced on to a bench-like contraption, his arms stretched out.

'You don't seem to understand,' Derek Samuels, his Head of Security, was saying smoothly, his face creased in feigned sympathy, as though he cared, as though he didn't enjoy it. 'I don't want to hurt you. It pains me to see you like this. But if you won't tell me what I want to know, I have no choice. The other guards here, they enjoy causing pain. I won't be able to stop them.'

The man's face contorted horribly as his arms were gradually pulled out of their sockets by the contraption he'd been connected to.

'I'll tell you nothing,' he managed to say through clenched teeth. 'You can't do this. It's illegal. The Authorities –'

'The Authorities don't care about you,' Derek said soothingly. 'You're beyond the law; Pincent Pharma security guards are sanctioned by the Anti-Terrorism Department to use whatever means necessary to get information out of Underground operatives. I can do what I want with you. And I will, believe me.'

He motioned to another guard, who was controlling the machine, and the prisoner screamed as his arms were pulled further away from his body.

'I just need to know where I can find the Underground's headquarters. It's an easy enough question,' Derek said, shaking his head sadly. 'Tell me that and you'll be free to go.'

The prisoner looked at him with wild eyes. 'Never,' he shouted. 'Never.'

Derek nodded and left the room; moments later the door next to Richard opened and Derek's face appeared.

'What do you want me to do?' he asked.

Richard sighed. Why didn't people realise that he would not be crossed? Why did they insist on fighting him when it was inevitable that they would lose? Did the Underground really think that they could make even a dent in his company's success? Did they really think that he would let them score even one point over him? 'Transfer him to the research lab,' he said with a shrug. 'I'm sure his organs will tell us more than he will.'

'Right you are.' Derek left and reappeared on the other side of the glass. 'You're going to research,' he said coolly.

'Research?' the prisoner stared at him. 'What do you mean?'

'I mean that since you're not talking, you're no

good to us. But luckily, your body can still be useful. They're going to have your organs. We need organs to test on, you see; cells to examine. The idea is that once you've been cut open, the scientists will get more out of you than I managed to.'

'Cut open?' The prisoner's face whitened visibly. 'You can't do that. I have rights. I have . . .'

Richard Pincent couldn't resist leaving his cubicle, throwing open the door to look at the prisoner in person. 'You have nothing,' he said, approaching the wooden bench from behind, causing the prisoner to jump. 'You are pathetic. You tried, and failed, to destroy Longevity this morning, just as the Underground will always fail. Now I am going to show you what happens to people who cross Richard Pincent. I am going to destroy you.'

'Who are you? Where's your humanity?' the prisoner shouted desperately.

Richard looked at him curiously. 'My humanity? I'm not the one trying to destroy life; you are, with your raids on Longevity.'

'I have a wife. Please, don't do this,' the man begged.

'More fool her,' Derek said thinly, as more guards appeared to help him transport the prisoner, 'for marrying a loser like you.'

Richard Pincent had seen enough; he walked out of the room, ignoring the screams of the prisoner, and made his way upstairs to his office. Once there, he went over to his window, pulling back the thick, velvet curtains to look outside. His office suite, over two hundred square metres with double-height ceilings that caused people to gasp when they entered it for the first time, was situated on the third floor of Pincent Pharma, overlooking the Thames. He had chosen its position carefully – too high and the view would have missed the river completely, too low and the buildings on the other side of the river would have blocked his light. Here, his view was perfect. Here, he was constantly reminded how important he was, how successful. Here, he was never in any doubt that the years he had spent coercing, charming and tramping on others had truly paid dividends, that his efforts had been worthwhile.

As he sat down at his desk, contemplating this thought, the phone rang and he picked it up. Few people had a direct line to this phone: only those who were useful to Richard, only those who could help him in some way.

'Richard Pincent.'

'Richard, it's Adrian.'

'Adrian. How are you?'

Adrian Barnet was the Deputy Secretary General, the second in command at the Authorities. A small, squat man, Adrian had been at university with Richard. The two of them had been friends of sorts; they still were, in so far as Richard considered anyone a friend.

'The attacks on Longevity,' Adrian said, his voice anxious. 'Are they set to continue, do you think?'

Adrian couldn't know about the raid that morning. The Authorities were always several steps behind, which suited Richard perfectly. 'They were isolated incidents,' he said carefully. 'Naturally, we've upped our security measures. I think you'll find there will be no more problems of that nature.'

'It's just that there have been questions raised,' Adrian continued. 'Concerns that any problem, or perceived problem, with the supply of Longevity knocks confidence. You know that the twenty points lost from the Finance Index last month are being directly attributed to the problems Pincent Pharma ran into.'

'Not problems,' Richard said immediately, grimacing as he spoke. 'Short-term blips which have been resolved. Our vulnerabilities have been eradicated.'

'The thing is, Richard, people are talking. The name of your grandson kept coming up this morning. People feel uncomfortable with your decision to offer him a job. They're concerned about his Underground connections, his association with the Surplus girl. He's dangerous. The worry is that he spent his formative years being brainwashed by her family . . .'

'That's the worry, is it?' Richard said icily. As he spoke, he pressed a button and a screen came to life, revealing Peter in the laboratory with Dr Edwards.

'It's just that your grandson is a figurehead for revolutionary activity,' Adrian continued, not noticing the sarcasm in Richard's voice. 'According to the Anti-Terrorism Department, the rebels are calling him the father of the next generation. Him and that Surplus girl.'

'The father of the next generation?' Richard almost spat the words. 'Well, Adrian, if that's what he is, tell me, where would you have him – free to roam the streets, associating with Underground scum, or here, at Pincent Pharma, where I can track his every move? Do you think I'm stupid, Adrian? Do you think that I am a fool?'

'No!' Adrian said quickly. 'No, of course not. But you can see how people might wonder –'

'No, Adrian, I cannot see,' Richard said angrily. 'But I will tell you one thing. If you think that I am going to let anyone – Peter, your Authorities colleagues, *anyone* – get in the way of Pincent Pharma, then you have another thing coming. Do you understand?'

'Yes, of course, I –'

'Peter is working for me now,' Richard interrupted. 'And when he signs the Declaration and embraces Longevity, the Underground movement will crumble.'

'He's signing the Declaration?' Adrian gasped.

'Of course he will,' Richard said dismissively. He hadn't broached the subject with Peter yet, but he was entirely sure he would convince him. Richard could be very persuasive when he chose to be.

'But he's a Surplus. Was, I mean . . .'

Richard allowed himself a little smile. 'Yes, he was. And now he isn't. Now he can live for ever if he chooses, and he will choose to, Adrian. Have you forgotten the power of Longevity to seduce?' he asked softly. 'Have you forgotten what it is to have temptation put in front of you, offered up on a platter? Peter won't be able to resist.'

There was a pause. 'So . . . what's he doing? Peter, I mean. Where have you got him working, if you don't mind me asking?'

'I do mind,' Richard replied levelly, 'but since you ask, I have him working with Dr Edwards. He's going to learn all about Longevity. All about its powers.'

'Dr Edwards. Isn't he the one who was moved off production?'

'He wasn't able to cope with modernisation,' Richard said smoothly. 'But he's still useful. Still the best teacher at Pincent Pharma. He's been heading up ReTraining for years now; he loves Longevity more than anyone in the world. If anyone can convince Peter to sign the Declaration, it's Dr Edwards. He sees the beauty of it. It's a religion to him.'

'You make him sound like your Mephistopheles.'

'Adrian, what I am offering Peter is eternal life, not a pact with the devil.'

'And you really think Peter will be swayed? It sounds risky to me.'

'Adrian, you are a civil servant,' Richard said coolly. 'Everything sounds risky to you. Trust me, Peter won't be able to resist the lure of eternal life. People have sold their souls for less.'

'You still believe in souls?' Adrian asked with a nervous laugh.

'What's not to believe? After all, our job here is to preserve souls, Adrian. Everyone's souls are now reliant on Pincent Pharma for their very existence.'

Adrian hesitated, apparently unsure whether or not Richard was joking. 'Don't let anyone else from the Authorities hear you say that,' he said nervously. 'I'm sure they think souls are their remit.'

'The Authorities think that everything is their remit,' Richard said, his tone suddenly icy. 'They're wrong.'

Chapter Five

Reluctantly pulling himself out of bed, Jude opened the curtains and looked outside. The sky was filled with ugly, dirty clouds; outside, neighbours offered each other half-smiles as they went about their business. What a grim place, he found himself thinking, a prison with no walls, a life sentence that kept repeating itself. No one was happy, no one was anything; they just were. It was really incredibly boring.

He looked down at the road for a few minutes, his mouth curling up in disgust, then he closed the curtains again and pulled himself off his bed, reluctantly replacing his warm duvet with two jumpers and a donkey jacket. Then, heavily, he ambled downstairs. The newspaper was on the doormat and he glanced at it briefly, skimming stories about the growing economy owing its success to the Authorities' ReTraining programme; about selfish energy-wasters causing a blackout in Manchester the day before; about the new craze for cliff-jumping and the dangers of having inadequate equipment. Nothing about the raid on Pincent Pharma, of course, he noticed wryly.

The Authorities would have covered that one up. He might find out more online, though; online newspapers weren't quite so easy for the Authorities to silence – they didn't depend on the Authorities for a permit to print, to use up valuable resources. You had to rely on blogs and transient websites for any real information.

He frowned briefly as he read, then noticed a leaflet that had been put through his door. Junk mail. Sighing, he picked it up, scanning it as he walked into the kitchen. The leaflet was cheaply produced and ink rubbed off on to his fingers. In spite of the cost of production, leaflets like this had become more commonplace recently – rabid rants from unhappy citizens on issues Jude cared very little about: longer sabbaticals for the over 150s, heating subsidies for the poor, better transport links. They were generally delivered in the dead of night, but there was very little point to them as far as Jude could see – no action suggested, no public meeting organised. He supposed that wasn't the point; the point was simply to be heard, which the complainants rarely were, since the leaflets always piled up in recycling bins.

This one, however, seemed to have set its sights rather higher. 'Longevity is murder' it proclaimed boldly across the top. His attention caught for a few seconds, Jude read a little more. 'Cliff-jumping no more than an "official" explanation for the rise in suicides' the leaflet shouted in large, capital letters. 'Longevity is killing us. And it's not just here. All

59

around the world, energy shortages are leading to death and disease because the UK won't give out Longevity for free.'

Jude frowned at the lack of logic. 'So Longevity is murder but you still want it given away for free?' he said dismissively to no one in particular before throwing both leaflet and paper away and opening the fridge, which reminded him silkily that he was running low on milk and other dairy products, and reminded him not to hold the door open for too long.

Closing the fridge and grabbing a banana from the fruit bowl, he left the kitchen and returned to his bedroom, the only room in the house that he really used; once there he turned on his computer. It took only seconds to spring to life; Jude had long ago wiped it clean of any unnecessary programmes, or files that might impede its speed; he could run his computer for twenty-four hours at the same level of energy usage as a low-energy light bulb. He regularly heard news reports that the Computer Age was dead because people couldn't afford the energy and it always made him laugh. It just reinforced his opinion of old people – that they were stupid and ignorant, that age still rotted the brain, whatever they said about Longevity.

He decided to take another quick look at Pincent Pharma – a week had gone by since he'd witnessed the Underground raid and every day he'd returned to see if there was any new activity, but there was nothing to see, just the perimeter guard completing a crossword, a food lorry arriving with supplies. Was Peter inside, he wondered. Was he standing by one of those many windows, looking out perhaps?

He stared at the image for a few minutes, then, navigating away from Pincent Pharma's security system, Jude idly began to search for the Underground's own network. It took him less than an hour to locate it, and when he did he was not surprised to find that it was less sophisticated than Pincent Pharma's. What did surprise him – and impress him – was that it was more difficult to access, mainly because it was messier, more ad hoc, with strands upon strands and no obvious central holding system. Without questioning his motives too deeply, he started to delve inwards. It took him nearly three hours, but lightly, delicately, he eventually found his way in, deftly overcoming security codes, teasing out hidden pages until, finally, he was where he wanted to be.

And then something occurred to him. He suddenly knew why he was there, knew what he wanted to do. He wanted to be part of it, wanted to show them what he could do. Peter had relied on the Underground's help all his life; Jude would instead help the Underground. One-nil to him. Yes, he thought to himself excitedly, he was going to offer his services. And they'd be stupid not to jump at the chance of having him. After all, what he didn't know about security networks wasn't worth knowing.

Allowing a little smile to creep on to his lips, he opened a message page and started to type.

Jude2124: Reporting for duty. See my CV below. I'm at your disposal. A friend. (PS your security needs an upgrade.)

He didn't have to wait long for a reply.

Hold1: Jude2124, please explain your presence here. We have you based in London, right?

Jude was impressed. They were more advanced than he'd thought, tracking him in under three minutes. Unfortunately for them, he smiled to himself, they'd have tracked him to a divert address on the other side of the city.

Jude2124: Not bad. So anyway, I saw the attack at Pincent Pharma the other week. Have it on tape, if you're interested? I'm sure I could be very valuable to you.

This time he had to wait over ten minutes for a response.

Pip: You have tapes? What do you intend to do with them?

Jude stared at the screen. Was this really Pip or did everyone at the Underground use his name when messaging? Pip was the guy who ran the Underground, the guy who had a huge price on his head. It couldn't be him, Jude decided. Not really.

Jude2124: Nothing. They're yours.

Pip: And what do you want in return?

Jude2124: My usual rate's £3000. You can have them for free. I want to sign up.

Pip: Sign up? What do you mean?

Jude frowned in irritation.

Jude2124: I mean I want to join you guys. You know, fight the enemy, fight Longevity. I want to join the Underground.

Pip: We'll have to think about that.

Jude rolled his eyes. What was there to think about?

Jude2124: Think? Why? How long for?

Pip: Are you going to be around for the next hour?

Jude2124: Sure.

Pip: Good. Stay by your computer. We'll get back to you.

Jude watched as the words fizzled away before his eyes, and sighed in annoyance. There he was thinking the Underground were dynamic revolutionaries when really they were as bad as the Authorities with their paperwork and protocols. Paperwork and protocols were all his father ever spoke about when he was alive. Thought they were the most important thing in the whole world. Couldn't see that they were pointless pieces of crap that only existed to give people like him a job.

Slowly, he stood up and walked towards his window, opening the curtain just a fraction. An hour? He was offering them his services – what was there to think about?

Irritated, he returned to his computer and logged on to MyWorld. In MyWorld there were no Authorities, no Underground, no stupid protocols.

Just hot girls, young people and fun things to do. His girlfriend was waiting for him on their bench; he sat down and told her about the Underground.

'They're idiots,' she said, raising an eyebrow flirtatiously. 'They don't deserve you.'

'No, they don't,' Jude agreed wholeheartedly. 'So what's up with you, anyway?'

He allowed himself to melt into the virtual embrace of his girlfriend, before wandering with her hand in hand across the park.

Jude froze as he felt an arm silently clamp around his neck; he didn't know how long he'd been lying down on a blanket, allowing chunks of milk chocolate to melt in his mouth. His girlfriend was still smiling at him expectantly on-screen.

'You wanted to meet,' a voice said. 'So here we are.'

'Please place your palm print on the screen, then move forward to retrieve your tray.'

Peter hesitated, tempted to rebel as he always was when he was told what to do, even by a machine, then, relenting, he did as the tinny voice requested and waited for his tray to appear in the hatch in front of him. It was his second week at Pincent Pharma and things were beginning to feel more familiar.

He reached forward to take his tray, then studied the food contained within it. Today he had salmon with vegetables, a baked potato with plenty of butter, fruit crumble for pudding, and a large glass of unidentifiable liquid. Pincent Pharma's nutrition sensor was a more sophisticated version of the identi-card scanners, which dictated the food groups that everyone should consume each week. The nutrition sensor went further still; at each meal it analysed employees via their palm print to establish their daily nutritional requirements according to their genetic profile and current metabolic status. Today, just as every day in the past week and a half, Peter's analysis revealed that he was slightly underweight and that he was lacking in various amino acids and sub-vitamins; those not present in the food were provided via the nutria-liquid. Dr Edwards looked at his own tray with a wry smile – it displayed a smaller piece of salmon, vegetables but no potato, a similar-looking liquid and no fruit crumble.

'After you,' he said, and followed Peter into the huge dining hall. Peter disliked this place – his only experience of communal eating on anything approaching this scale had been the far smaller Central Feeding at Grange Hall where the Surpluses had eaten each meal silently, carefully, knowing that any transgression of the rules would result in a beating or some other punishment. And whilst the Pincent Pharma dining hall had no such penalties – employees talked freely, eyes were not cast down-wards, and a spill was greeted with sympathy not fear – the hair on the back of Peter's neck still stiffened whenever he entered it.

Seeing an empty table on the other side of the

dining hall, he walked towards it, but as he made his way past all the other tables, something caused him to stop. Someone, in fact. A woman in a lab coat, talking loudly to the people around her.

'The whole idea of Surpluses having rights is illogical. The most basic human right is the right to life, and Surpluses have forfeited that, so to talk about welfare or other so-called basic rights is nonsense, pure and simple.'

'Yes, but once a Surplus has been created, is the contravention really its fault?' a man interjected. 'After all, it was the parent who made the choice, who contravened the law. I think there is an argument for one of the parents losing their life, and allowing the Surplus to live.'

'Which parent?' the woman said dismissively. 'How could you decide? No, knowingly or otherwise, Surpluses are a contravention of the Declaration and they have to pay for it. I'm sorry, but that's the only way.'

Peter was standing behind the woman and gradually all her companions turned to stare at him. It took her a minute or so to realise that they were not staring at her, and she shifted in her seat to discover what had attracted their attention.

When she saw Peter, she blushed slightly, then, as if determined to regain her composure, stuck out her chin.

'It's Peter, isn't it?' she asked coolly.

Peter nodded.

'Well, Peter. I'm sorry if you didn't like what you

just heard, but these things have to be said. Rules are rules.'

Peter nodded tightly. He couldn't make a scene, he knew that. He just had to walk away. But he'd never been very good at walking away. 'Rules,' he said. 'Right.'

He was fixed to the spot; he felt Dr Edwards come up behind him and put a hand on his shoulder. Then his teacher turned to the woman.

'Perhaps these things are a matter of opinion. I'm not sure that Surpluses have any debt to pay. Their existence is not of their doing, after all.'

The woman looked disconcerted by Dr Edwards' intervention. 'That's not what the Declaration says,' she said irritably. 'It's not a matter of opinion at all. You should know – after all, you're a scientist. Isn't science all black and white?'

Dr Edwards smiled gently. 'Ah, but that's just the thing. Science teaches us that we are rarely right. The whole discipline of science is aimed at proving ourselves wrong, is it not?'

The woman looked at him archly. 'You're very outspoken for a scientist who's been demoted to ReTraining,' she said coolly. 'Then again, I suppose that's why you're where you are. But all the same, I'd think before opening your mouth if all you can do is come out with subversive rants about your views on Surpluses. Not everyone will be as tolerant as we are.'

'Tolerant?' Dr Edwards asked. 'Is that what you are?'

'Yes,' she said thinly. 'And I notice the Surplus himself isn't saying anything.'

Peter bristled, and he gripped his lunch tray, barely able to control himself.

'Peter is not a Surplus,' Dr Edwards said quietly. 'He is an employee of this company, and he deserves a little more respect.'

'Yes, I know he's an employee. That's why this conversation started.' The woman stared at Dr Edwards for a moment, then her eyes flicked over to the camera in the corner. 'We all know his mother's in prison,' she said, her voice quieter all of a sudden. 'You know that he's here because Richard Pincent is his grandfather and felt sorry for him?'

'She's not my mother,' Peter growled, under his breath, moving towards the woman angrily. 'And I don't care where she is.'

Dr Edwards grimaced and motioned for Peter to stay where he was.

'He is here because he has a contribution to make,' he said, his voice low. 'Unless you doubt Mr Pincent's motives? And it is probably not that advisable to go round denouncing his mother. After all, she is Mr Pincent's daughter.'

The woman's eyes flickered upwards again, this time towards the bank of cameras positioned along the walls of the dining hall, and she flushed slightly. 'I was not denouncing her,' she said, a slight note of stress in her voice. 'I was just . . . stating a fact. But you're right, of course. The boy is not a Surplus any more, and I'm sure he's a very good addition to Pincent Pharma.' She managed a smile of sorts, then turned back to her dining companions; Peter and Dr Edwards began to walk away.

The woman, though, had not finished. 'Although you can't say the same for the other one. The girl,' she said, her voice quieter, but still audible to Peter. 'Does she deserve my respect too? We're getting firm on immigrant labour and then we just allow Surpluses to escape and make them Legal. What's to respect?'

'Ignore her,' Dr Edwards whispered, but Peter barely heard him. Anger was shooting up and down his body like fireworks, propelling him forward until he was right beside the woman.

'Don't you ever mention Anna again,' he said, his voice low, leaning down so that his face was close to the woman's. 'That's her name. Anna. And if you ever, ever bring her up in conversation again, I will not be responsible for my actions.'

The woman looked at him and feigned thin laughter. 'I think you're making my point for me, Peter,' she said, shaking her head, and raising her eyebrows at the man next to her. 'Youth is ignorance. It's all take, take, take. Aggression instead of discussion. Perhaps you'll learn in time, but I imagine in your case it really will take a long time. Once a Surplus . . .'

She shook her head, a look of pity in her eye. Peter's heart, meanwhile, was pounding in his chest and every instinct made him want to throw himself at the woman, to make her understand what it felt like to be labelled Surplus, to be subjugated, beaten down, humiliated, until all you knew was the desire to serve, to pay your debt to society, to beg forgiveness over and over again simply for existing – to feel like Anna had for most of her life.

Instead, he forced himself to stand up straight, to look away.

'There, you see. He doesn't have anything to say now,' the woman said triumphantly, picking up her fork and delicately swirling some spaghetti round it.

Dr Edwards moved to guide Peter away. 'I imagine Peter has plenty to say,' he interjected, smiling drily, 'but now is probably not the time, wouldn't you agree?' Carefully, he steered Peter away from the table and towards another on the other side of the hall.

They sat down and started eating in silence. When their meal was almost finished, finally trusting himself to speak, Peter looked up at Dr Edwards.

'What did she mean about your views on Surpluses?' he asked. 'You don't think Surpluses have a debt to pay society?'

Dr Edwards put down his knife and fork and looked around hesitantly, then leant in closer towards Peter. 'No, Peter, I don't believe that Surpluses have a debt to pay. I think, on the contrary, that we probably owe a debt to them.' His voice was low and soft, inaudible to anyone but Peter.

Peter eyed him cautiously. 'You do? So why don't they?'

Dr Edwards took a mouthful of food and chewed it

silently, then put down his fork. 'Peter,' he said, his voice a little louder than before, 'try to understand that the way people respond to you isn't personal. People have always been fearful of youth. Children and young people are threatening – they challenge things, they reject the status quo. Even before Longevity was invented, teenagers were being demonised by society. They were being issued with civil behaviour orders limiting their movements, they were being blamed for crime, for society's ills. As people started to have fewer children, so the fear of young people grew. The further away from something we are, the more we tend to mistrust it, Peter. We dislike the unknown, we reject anything alien to us: people with views that contradict ours, societies that are run along very different lines. And children are very different. Young people always contradict their elders – it's in their nature.'

'You're saying they're scared of me?' Peter's tone was sarcastic, dismissive.

'I'm saying that you unsettle them. I'm saying that if you want to make friends, you will have to be patient with them. Prove to them that they have no reason to fear you.'

'You don't fear me.'

'No, Peter, I don't,' Dr Edwards said, a little twinkle in his eye. 'I rather enjoy being contradicted. It forces me to think harder.'

Peter digested this for a few seconds, then shrugged. 'I don't need friends. I've never had friends.'

'I doubt that, Peter. And remember you're fighting over a hundred years of doctrine, of public relations, of the almost total absence of youth,' Dr Edwards said, looking up at him seriously. 'You can't expect people to understand staight away.'

'I don't expect people to understand at all,' Peter said angrily. 'I just want them to leave us alone. I want everyone to just leave us alone.'

Chapter Six

Jude felt a trickle of sweat roll down towards his eye and he shook it off. He had often imagined what it would feel like to be captured, to be imprisoned and tortured for information – he'd imagined the adrenaline rush, the feeling of emergency that he knew it would entail. He'd quizzed his father on torture techniques employed by the Authorities; hadn't really believed him when his father had said that torture wasn't part of the protocol.

Now, though, as he sat on his chair with his hands tied behind his back, he didn't feel an adrenaline rush. He felt fear, desperation. But he was determined not to show it. He was a fighter. He wouldn't let them get to him that easily.

'Interesting system you've got here.' The man talking was tall, medium build. Behind him was another man. He was unshaven, his hair tousled, his clothes nondescript, but Jude immediately recognised him. It was his eyes that gave him away; the bright blue colour, the intensity of them that was both terrifying and reassuring at once. He'd seen them on pictures, had heard people talk about them, about the man they belonged to. Pip, the most wanted man in Britain. Pip, the man who in some tales had secret powers, who conspiracy theorists claimed was working for the Authorities to help flush out any dissidents. The man who had evaded capture for years.

'You came?' he asked, his voice constricting as he spoke, forcing him to clear his throat several times. 'Just like that?'

'Just like that,' Pip said. 'Weren't you expecting us?'

Jude gulped. 'Not you,' he said. 'I've seen your face. I mean, you're just here, in my room . . .'

The other man chuckled. 'He's right. He's seen our faces. I guess that means we'll have to kill him.'

Jude's face went white, then he shook himself. 'Look, I'm on your side. I'm not the enemy.'

'And what side's that, Jude?' It was Pip talking. His voice was low, soft, almost hypnotic.

Jude cleared his throat again nervously. He'd never wanted to fit in anywhere before but now, in front of Pip, he wanted acceptance, and it scared him. 'You're the Underground,' he said. 'You're the resistance.'

'Freedom fighters, eh? And what are we fighting for, exactly?' Pip was smiling slightly, and it unsettled Jude.

'You're against Longevity, aren't you? Against old people.' His voice was shaking a little.

'Against old people.' The smile deepened. 'That's interesting. And why do you want to join us?'

Jude looked at him uncertainly. 'I thought you'd be

grateful for my help.'

'How old are you?' Pip leant in close; Jude could feel his breath on his ear.

'Old enough.' It was all he could do not to whimper pathetically.

Pip moved away suddenly, and the other man spoke. 'And who taught you how to hack into systems?'

Jude felt himself relax slightly. They were on more comfortable ground now. He could talk about hacking for hours. 'I taught myself. I got a computer when I was really young and I used to –'

'Nice house, this,' the man interrupted, throwing Jude off his stride. 'Big for just one person.'

'It was my mum's. She –'

'And you're Legal,' the man interrupted again.

'You don't think the neighbours might have reported me if I wasn't?'

The man, who had noticed the sarcasm in his voice, regarded him coolly, then moved around to face Jude so their noses were almost touching. 'You may think that you're very clever, but we do not appreciate people hacking into our systems, leaving trails for others to find. Do you understand?'

'I didn't leave a trail,' Jude protested. 'I never do.'

'And yet we found you,' Pip said gently. 'We always leave a trail, Jude, whether we wish to or not.'

Jude reddened. He must have messed up his diversion code. A stupid mistake.

'You didn't go to South America. Why?'

Jude stared at Pip. 'What?'

'When your mother went. You could have gone too.'

'How did you know . . .' Jude started to say then stopped. 'So you know who I am. Why bother asking any questions then?'

Pip smiled. 'It's nice to hear it first-hand, I suppose.'

Jude sighed. 'Like I was going to move halfway across the world,' he said dismissively. 'Anyway, I wasn't that wild on her new husband.' As he spoke, an image of his mother crept into his head and he forced it out again. He didn't care about her. Didn't care that she'd followed that creep to South America after his father died. He could take care of himself anyway.

'So this is your life now? Hacking into systems, blackmailing companies?' It was the other man talking again. Jude bristled.

'It's not blackmail. I offer a service. I only hack in to show them their systems are open to threats.'

'Threats like you?'

Jude didn't say anything. This wasn't turning out at all as he'd planned it.

'Show me the tapes,' the man said briskly. 'Now.'

Jude opened up his DVD rewriter and handed the man a disk.

'This the only copy?'

'Uh-huh.'

'If we find out there are more, you'll regret it.'

Jude's usual insouciance seemed to have deserted

him. 'So can I join?' he asked, his voice hoarse, nervous. 'Did I pass the test?' He looked at Pip hopefully; Pip laughed.

'Test?' he said, walking towards the door. 'The only tests worth passing are the ones we set ourselves,' he said, turning briefly. 'You will choose your path, or perhaps it will choose you. Either way, I expect that we will meet again. Until then, be careful Jude. You know about Icarus?'

Jude nodded quickly, as though showing his knowledge might impress Pip, might change his mind. 'Sure. Flew too close to the sun.'

Pip nodded and, to Jude's immense disappointment, turned and made his way out of the room. 'And singed his wings, Jude,' he said as he walked. 'And singed his wings.'

Dr Edwards didn't mention the lunchtime incident again. Once back at the lab, Peter went back to learning about enzymes and their role in the body; Dr Edwards went back to his research. They worked silently, the only words exchanged ones of necessity.

But later that afternoon, Dr Edwards called him over.

'Peter, come and look at this.' Dr Edwards lifted his head from the large microscope in front of him and moved out of the way, motioning for Peter to take his place and peer through the lens. Slowly, Peter wandered over and did as Dr Edwards bid.

'What do you see?'

Peter shrugged. 'I dunno,' he said casually. He was still feeling resentful, had found nowhere to direct his anger except at whatever was in front of him.

'Look carefully,' Dr Edwards instructed him. 'You might need to focus it a little to really see clearly.'

Peter reluctantly moved closer to the microscope and rested his head on it, allowing his eyes to adjust to the magnification.

'Do you see the cell?' Dr Edwards asked. 'You should be able to pick out its nucleus.'

Peter studied the almost transparent blob, magnified several thousand times. Then he squinted and realised that the blob was in fact two blobs. One small blob on the left with a clear, dark centre, and a larger mass on the right. He nodded.

'Describe it to me.'

'Transparent. Uh . . .' Peter stared at the blob on the left, trying to work out what he should be seeing.

'Shape? Edges?'

'Round. No, slightly oblong. Edges are . . . a bit ragged.'

'Good. Now, back to the colour. Any tinges of colour?'

Peter frowned. 'Yellowish,' he said. 'A tinge of yellow, anyway. Dark yellow.'

'Does it look healthy?'

'I don't know. I haven't learnt . . .'

'Forget learning. Does it look healthy to you? Gut reaction.'

'No. No, it doesn't. It looks . . . tired.'

'Good,' Dr Edwards encouraged him. 'Tired just about sums it up. Now, watch what happens when I do this.'

Peter watched as a long, thin glass instrument appeared in his view. The instrument deposited a drop of liquid on the small, sickly-looking blob, then disappeared out of view. Immediately, Peter saw the blob change. From a pasty-looking off-yellow colour, the blob became a brighter white colour, almost shining in its translucence. Its edges began to smooth, and in the centre, a core became visible, like an egg yolk but white, even whiter than the rest. The entire process took just a few seconds.

'That,' breathed Dr Edwards, 'is Renewal.'

'Renewal,' Peter said flatly.

'Yes, Peter. Cells Renewed, reborn. The power of Longevity, you see, is not to make the old last longer, but to make it young again. That is the miracle, Peter, that all of this is about, unfolding right before your eyes. Cells being reborn, returning to their initial state, in just a few seconds. Pretty impressive, huh?'

'I thought you were on the side of Surpluses. I thought you liked young people?' Peter muttered.

Dr Edwards looked at him for a moment, then lowered his voice. 'Peter, there is a difference between a thing and its implementation. Longevity drugs, the Renewal process, are the most exciting scientific development the world has ever seen. It's beautiful, perfect in its simplicity. Surpluses are one of the Authorities' policies. The two are not entwined.'

'Except they are, aren't they?' Peter said. He met Dr Edwards' eyes, saw them flinch slightly, then he turned back to the microscope. 'So it works with all cells? Why do people still have wrinkles?'

'It works best with organs,' Dr Edwards said after a pause. 'We can Renew other cells, but only on Petri dishes, not whilst they are . . . in situ. Skin is one of the more difficult areas for us. But organs are the most important. They are what keep us alive.'

Peter stared for a few more seconds, then looked up.

'And my cells. They're like the white one, are they?'

Dr Edwards nodded. 'That's right. Young, dynamic and healthy.'

'So nature creates new cells too. Only it does it by creating new people, not by renewing old ones.'

Dr Edwards' mouth attempted a smile. 'I suppose so, but what you're seeing here is nature's strength being harvested.'

'You think that's a good thing?' Peter asked, turning back to the microscope, his eyes flickering up to watch Dr Edwards' expression. 'You never wanted children.' It was a statement, not a question, but Dr Edwards moved back slightly, his eyes moving involuntarily towards the cameras on the ceiling.

'Me? Have children? No, no I didn't. I couldn't. Science has always been my child. It required all my energy. All my time.'

'Science?' Peter sounded more incredulous than he'd intended, more dismissive.

Dr Edwards shrugged. 'Many years ago people used to talk about the miracle of childbirth, the miracle of new life. But I see that miracle every day – the miracle of Renewal, of rebirth. And it's a safer choice, I think, than creating life. Children are more demanding than science. They enslave you; they take away your freedom.'

Peter looked away. Children were demanding. Ben absorbed far more of Anna's time than Peter had anticipated, made her exhausted all the time, took all her attention. But that wasn't a reason not to have them. Children were the future. They had to be.

'What I'm trying to explain to you, Peter,' Dr Edwards continued gently, 'is that nature and Longevity are not mutually exclusive. Humans are able to adapt very well to new situations.'

Peter thought for a moment. He'd never thought of Longevity as beautiful, as a miracle. And he'd thought that Pincent Pharma would be full of people like the woman at lunch, not thoughtful and kind like Dr Edwards. Then he shook himself. He was here to do a job, and he was going to do it.

'So this is how it works,' he said, squinting at the cells. 'But how? What's in the liquid you put on the cell? And what happens to the liquid? I mean, Longevity drugs are tablets, aren't they? How do you convert the liquid into tablets?'

'More questions. You know that curiosity killed the cat?' Peter started slightly and swung round to find his grandfather standing a few feet behind him.

'Curiosity also makes a great student,' Dr Edwards said.

Richard Pincent shrugged. 'There's plenty of time for studying, though,' he said easily. 'One thing we all have is plenty of time, isn't that right, Peter?'

Peter nodded awkwardly.

'If you sign the Declaration, I mean,' his grandfather continued, his eyes boring into Peter's. 'You are signing, aren't you?'

Peter cleared his throat. Pip's notes had briefed him on this question; they'd told him to say he was signing. But now, standing in front of his grandfather, he found couldn't say it. Wouldn't say it.

'I wasn't planning to, no,' he said.

'I see.' His grandfather nodded, his eyes darkening. 'In that case, perhaps you'd like to come with me?'

Chapter Seven

Peter followed his grandfather down the corridor in silence, trying to ignore his heart thudding loudly in his chest. They took the lift up to the third floor, which was empty but for patrolling guards, luxurious but for the heavy locks on heavy-looking doors.

'And this is my office,' his grandfather said, eventually, keying in a code which opened a large door. 'Changes every day, this code,' his grandfather said, noticing Peter's staring eyes. 'Best security system in the whole world.'

Peter nodded silently, and only just stopped himself from gasping as he looked around. The room was opulent in a way that Peter had never seen before: polished floorboards covered with heavy rugs, ceilings high enough for three men to stand on each other's shoulders, lights everywhere – embedded in the ceiling, standard lamps, side lights, lights in cupboards, lights on the floor. It was warm, too – a fire crackled under a huge mantelpiece and he immediately imagined Anna curled up comfortably in front of it, reading. She'd love it, he thought to himself bitterly. But the thing that drew Peter's eyes, the thing that made this room bigger, better, more incredible than any other room he'd been in, was the view – of the river, of London. The window behind his grandfather's desk was enormous and – incredibly – it could be opened, something his grandfather appeared to take great delight in demonstrating.

'We do things differently here, Peter,' he said, his eyes glinting. 'The rules that apply to others don't apply to us.'

Peter cleared his throat, trying his best to appear relaxed and confident, but underneath the facade, he was filled with a sense of dread – dread that he was going to be expelled from Pincent Pharma before he'd been of any use to the Underground, dread that he'd allowed his heart to rule his head, stupidly, foolishly.

'So, Peter,' his grandfather said, sitting down at his large, mahogany desk and motioning for Peter to take the chair on the other side of it. 'How are you getting on?'

Peter looked at him cautiously and forced a smile. 'Fine. I'm getting on fine.'

Richard Pincent nodded. 'Fine. I see.' He sat back in his chair. Peter's eyes had been darting about the room curiously, and he made himself look down instead. Anna had told him before that his eyes were dangerous – they unsettled people, they refused to compromise. 'But you've decided not to sign the Declaration.'

Peter bit his lip. 'Actually,' he said, his throat

feeling suddenly dry, 'I haven't really decided. I'm . . . thinking about it.' Inside, he knew he was doing the right thing; he still felt slightly sick even suggesting he might sign.

'Peter, I wonder if you'd let me tell you the story of Longevity.'

Peter looked up briefly. 'I know the story,' he said, before he could stop himself. 'I saw the film.'

His grandfather held his gaze for a few seconds. 'Indulge me, Peter, just for a few minutes?'

Peter nodded quickly, kicking himself.

'The story of Longevity,' his grandfather said, standing up and walking towards the vast window behind him, 'starts many thousands of years ago, when humans first walked this earth.'

Peter found his eyes drawn back to the window and its spectacular view. Slowly, he scanned the horizon, taking in the buildings on the other side of the river, the river itself. Somewhere out there were his friends; somewhere out there were the other members of the Underground, his comrades. They were outside and they were depending on him, just like Anna had in Grange Hall. And just like then, he wasn't going to let anyone down.

'As soon as man worked out how to communicate, how to develop tools, the fight against death had begun. Man learnt how to protect himself from predators, to insulate himself against his environment. Through discovery, he extended his lifespan. But that wasn't enough, Peter.'

Peter nodded seriously. 'It wasn't?'

'No. Because man still feared death; feared disappearing into nothingness, feared how death made each life insignificant. And so he sought to attack the things that ended his life – disease and illness. Longevity did not appear out of nowhere, Peter; it is simply the latest invention in a long line of inventions – antibiotics, vaccinations, X-rays, even sanitation – all of which extended man's life substantially. If you reject Longevity, then why not reject all of medicine? If nature's way is the best way, then surely a bandage, antiseptic, any intervention at all in fact, is morally wrong, is "unnatural".'

Peter felt his cheeks redden. 'I haven't . . . I mean, I haven't rejected Longevity. I just haven't decided.'

His grandfather looked at him impatiently. 'Then decide, Peter,' he said, a hint of menace in his voice. 'Decide. Choose life, Peter. Man has always searched for eternal life – through religion, through philosophy. And you are being offered it on a platter.'

'Religion?' Peter frowned.

'You won't know much about religion, Peter; people have no need of it now,' he said. 'But people used to put great store by the notion of a god, or gods. Great men spent many hours debating the subtle nuances of different religions, arguing that belief in a higher being, in an afterlife, in redemption, placed humans above animals; that it made them special, superior. Great wars were fought between countries that held different religious beliefs, even when the points of contention were so small as to be laughable now. But religions were based on the pretext that humans were fallible, that humans died. Only gods lived for ever; only through religion could humans hope to achieve salvation and some sort of existence after death. Now, we ourselves live for ever. Now, Peter, we are our own gods. Through Longevity, we are more powerful than anything man has ever imagined.'

Peter cleared his throat. 'I heard,' he said carefully, 'that religion was suppressed by the Authorities because its leaders didn't agree with Longevity.'

His grandfather's eyes clouded over and Peter kicked himself for speaking his mind yet again. 'It's true enough that religious leaders condemned Longevity,' his grandfather said darkly. 'But why do you think that was, Peter? I'll tell you why. It was because they were desperate to hold on to power and influence. Do you think people miss being told what to do, being encouraged to mistrust others because they happened to believe in a different god? Do you think people miss the corruption, the genocide, the wars, the terrorist attacks that were all implemented in the name of some god or other? Do you think they are sorry to be free of all of this? To make their own decisions?'

Peter said nothing, and his grandfather smiled triumphantly. 'Of course,' he said lightly, 'personally, I'm rather grateful to religion. You see, we used to be rather behind the US when it came to scientific research; everyone expected their scientists to come up with something like Longevity, not us. But their religious leaders banned research on stem cells. Banned it – can you believe that? So their research dried up. We took the baton, and . . . well, you know the rest.'

Peter frowned. He felt confused, didn't know what to say. 'There used to be young people,' he said eventually. 'Now there aren't any.'

His grandfather nodded. 'That's what people have chosen, Peter. There are difficult choices to be made and that was one that was unavoidable. But is it really such a bad thing?' He shook his head dismissively. 'These young people you talk of, they had nothing. No hope, no prospects. They were turning to crime to support themselves, Peter. They terrorised communities.'

He walked back to his desk, leaning against the front of it so that he was just inches away from Peter. 'And then we discovered Longevity. The Holy Grail, Peter. The secret to eternal life.'

Peter took a deep breath. 'And nature?'

'Nature?' His grandfather shook his head with disgust. 'Nature is our enemy, Peter. She has always been our enemy. Nature held sway over humankind, striking us down at will, ravaging our bodies with cancer, killing women during childbirth, creating plagues that wiped out entire cities. All these are the gifts of nature, Peter. She is no friend of humans.'

'And Longevity is?' Peter asked uncertainly.

'Yes, it is. Longevity was created to save us, Peter,' his grandfather said gravely. 'Imagine if Anna was dying. Wouldn't you want to give her Longevity then? Wouldn't you want to save her life? Yes or no?'

Peter didn't say anything for a second or two. 'I . . . I don't know,' he said. He realised as he spoke that he was telling the truth. Then he shook himself. It was a trick question. Wanting to save someone's life didn't make Longevity OK.

'No,' his grandfather smiled. 'I don't suppose you do. The truth of the matter is that nothing is black and white – it is all shades of grey. You might want to think about that before you throw your life away for a lost cause.'

As soon as Peter had left, Richard picked up the phone and dialled Adrian's private line.

'Adrian,' he said, when the phone was answered, 'where are we at with the research grants?'

'Grants?'

Richard frowned. It was a woman's voice.

'I'm sorry. I thought this was Adrian Barnet's line.'

'It was. Now it's my line. My name is Hillary Wright. I'm the new Deputy Secretary General.'

Richard took a few seconds to digest this information. 'And Adrian?'

'Adrian has been redeployed.'

Richard nodded. 'Then welcome to your post,' he said jovially. 'This is Richard Pincent speaking. Of Pincent Pharma.'

'Yes, I rather thought it might be.'

The voice wasn't cold, but it sounded almost amused; certainly she didn't sound impressed. One of the new breed of women, he realised irritably; the first generation of women with no expectation of raising young to hamper their ambition, to temper their choices.

Winning over the female population had been critical to the success and legalisation of Longevity. The Authorities had, predictably, failed miserably in convincing them, so it had been left to Richard to hire the slickest spin doctors, the most Machiavellian individuals he could find to win over the hearts and minds of Britain and then the world. 'Free from the slavery of child rearing' went the strapline aimed at women; eminent female academics had been secured to argue Longevity's case, to hail it as the ultimate triumph for women, the final emancipation. The strategy had been successful and soon women, unencumbered by the desire to have babies, focused their attentions on the workplace instead. The post-Longevity generation of women saw no glass ceilings; they soon found their way into company boardrooms, soon took over companies, public bodies, until no one thought twice about it. No one except Richard. This new breed of woman made him uncomfortable; made him nervous. They were known by those of his generation as 'the ball-breakers', but to Richard, the reality was more ominous. Ball-breakers didn't understand the codes and protocols of men; they were always so much harder to bribe, to meld. He would have to proceed carefully, cautiously.

'Well, you must come to the labs. I'd love to show you round,' he said coolly.

'Indeed,' Hillary replied. 'I wonder, would you mind telling me what you meant when you asked about grants? I hope you weren't attempting to bypass official channels?'

Richard bristled. 'Of course not,' he said quickly. 'I do apologise – I thought I was talking to Adrian.'

'You and Adrian discussed research grants?'

'No,' he said, feeling his anger grow. 'I just wanted him to put me in touch with the grant department.'

'Yes. Yes, I see.'

Richard felt a trickle of sweat make its way down the back of his neck.

'And how is your grandson getting on?' Hillary continued.

'Peter? He's doing well. Very well, in fact.'

'I'm pleased. We were talking about him yesterday, as it happens,' she said. 'Thought it might be a good idea to hold a press conference. Peter Pincent signs the Declaration at Pincent Pharma, something like that. It wouldn't be a bad thing to demonstrate once and for all that his links with the Underground have been severed.'

Richard cleared his throat, then let his neck drop backwards as he took a moment to think. He had always viewed life, including human relationships, as a game of chess: the trick was to think three steps ahead, to use people to their best advantage, to always have one eye on the final win, on the absolute conquest. But usually he knew his opponent. Right now, he felt unarmed.

'A press conference?' he asked carefully, sitting up straight again, asserting his dominance if only to himself. 'That's an interesting idea. But not one that we should rush into, I suspect.'

'Rush?' Hillary asked, her voice betraying nothing. 'No, nothing should be rushed. But I understand that Peter will be sent his Declaration shortly. So will the girl. The Authorities are keen to . . . tie up loose ends. And since I have no doubt that your grandson will be signing forthwith, I can't see that anyone is rushing, can you? We thought next week would be ideal. Perhaps you'd like to arrange it?'

'Next week?' The blood drained from Richard's face.

'Next week,' Hillary confirmed curtly. 'Now, there was another thing. Adrian's notes suggest that a new version of Longevity, Longevity 5.4, is finally ready for launch. Is this correct?'

Richard, still preoccupied by the idea of Peter signing the Declaration in front of the press in only one week's time, nodded vaguely. 'Longevity 5.4,' he said. 'Yes, that's right. But we prefer to call it Longevity+. Longevity, only better.'

'Indeed,' Hillary responded. 'The Authorities would like to see it released.'

'Or,' Richard said, spotting an opportunity, 'we

could launch Longevity+ at the same time that Peter signs his Declaration. Of course, next week will be too soon, I'm afraid – there's testing to be completed, details to be finalised. But we could look at a date some time next month instead?'

'Out of the question. Anyway, according to Adrian's notes, the testing has already been done. But I do like the idea of combining the two. Shall we set a date now? Which day next week suits you best?'

'*Some* testing has been done,' Richard said icily. 'There is still more to do.'

'Then we can make a preliminary announcement,' Hillary said.

'We?'

'We. After all, Richard, it is the Authorities' licence that has enabled the development of this drug, is it not? And it was the Authorities who granted Peter Legal status.'

Richard could feel himself getting hot. No one cornered Richard Pincent like this. No one. 'Peter was not *granted* Legal status by anyone,' he said tightly. '"A Life for a Life", remember. The Authorities didn't have any alternative. And next week is too soon. If you and I are going to announce anything, I need more time.'

There was a pause, then he thought he heard Hillary sigh. 'There is no more time,' she said, her voice a little less combative. 'The week after next sees the World Energy Forum. If we are to have any leverage, we need an announcement before then.'

Suddenly, Richard saw a chink in her armour. A chink that could mean he was back in control of the game. 'You're saying that you need Pincent Pharma to bail you out at the Forum, to give you negotiating power?'

'And you need me to approve the drug. To approve your methods.'

Richard paused. 'Our methods?'

'Adrian's notes are very enlightening. I just hope you're not contravening the Protection of Surpluses Bill, Richard. You'll know that corporate crime isn't tolerated by the Authorities.'

Richard took a deep breath. The Protection of Surpluses Bill had been a sop to the Liberals when the Surplus Halls were set up; everyone knew that it was meaningless – a series of checklists, of safeguards that everyone turned a blind eye to. But it was still on the Statute. If Hillary wanted to, she could insist its requirements were followed. Which meant that they were moving rapidly towards a stalemate situation, he realised. One that would suit neither of them. 'Perhaps we might work together on this one, Hillary,' he said carefully. 'I suppose a preliminary announcement might be possible.'

'Next week? And Peter will sign the Declaration?'

'Next week,' Richard smiled thinly. 'Friday. I'll arrange the conference for late afternoon, and perhaps you could visit us earlier in the day to see the production process for yourself?'

'Very well,' Hillary said curtly. 'Then I'll be in touch.'

Richard put the phone down and waited a few seconds before picking it up again and dialling a number. 'I need you to do something for me,' he said, when Derek Samuels answered. 'You know Underground message formats? I need one delivered. And it has to be utterly convincing . . . You can? Good, OK, then. Take this down word for word . . .'

His heart beating quickly, he relayed the message, explained what Samuels was to do with it. As he spoke, his eyes flicked up to the screen to his right, which was trained in on Dr Edwards' lab. 'Oh and Samuels?' he said. 'I've got another job for you. Delicate matter. I'll need one of your best operatives. Former Catcher would be ideal. They'd be good with former Surpluses, wouldn't they?'

'A former Surplus? You don't mean . . .'

Richard shook his head at the surprise in Samuels' voice. Did he really think that Richard Pincent would let emotion or something as meaningless as family get in the way of success?

'Actually, perhaps you'd better come up to my office. This is one I'd rather discuss in person.'

He switched the receiver off, then turned to his computer to bring up his profit ratios. Money and power – he had more of both than he'd ever imagined possible. And nothing – no one – was going to take it away from him.

Chapter Eight

Peter didn't sleep well that night. However much he tried to suppress them, the first notes of doubt had started to float into his head, clamouring to be heard, and leaving him angry and feeling guilty. He found himself wondering about religion, about the thin line between old-fashioned medicine and Longevity, and he found himself worrying about how much of an impact he could really make on the world in just fifty years, if he even lived that long. Fifty more years didn't seem much when everyone else was here for ever. Fifty years wasn't really long at all.

It was with relief, then, that Peter found the note from Pip on the doormat on his way to work the following morning, reminding him that he had an important role to play, that he was significant after all. At first he thought it was another flyer for some service or other – painting, decorating, vitamin injections, plastic surgery, petrol coupon trading schemes, permanent make-up – but as he started to crumple it in his hands, he saw the mark of the Underground – a small dove with an olive branch in its beak, representing the search for new life. Immediately he ducked back inside, carefully uncurling it.

Looking for a new direction? Bored of doing the same thing every day?

Call our recruitment consultants today to ask about our training. Whether you're interested in technology, languages, science or the service industry, we've got the job and training to make your dreams come true. If you believe in yourself, anything is possible.

Ring 0845 389 7053, where we're waiting to take your call.

It looked inconsequential, but Peter knew immediately that no one else on his road would have received this particular advert. Quickly, he raced upstairs and dug out the mobile phone that Pip had given him. Computer and standard phone lines couldn't be trusted, he'd told Peter. The Underground used old-fashioned mobiles tuned to unique frequencies which they changed regularly so that the Authorities weren't able to discover them. It took just one rashly made phone call from a landline or web phone to put the whole operation in jeopardy.

Peter dialled the number.

'Yes?'

He was fairly sure it was Pip, but he couldn't be certain; his tone was brisker than usual.

'I'm looking for a new direction,' Peter said,

reading the words straight off the flyer. 'I believe in myself.'

'Then our consultants can help. Grays Inn Road, number 87, eighth floor, room 24b, 6 p.m. tonight.'

Peter scribbled down the details. 'Great. I'll be there,' he said breathlessly, but already the phone had gone dead.

Later that morning, Ben was in a grizzly mood, and Anna fussed over him as she walked along the suburban streets, bending over his pram frequently to pull his blanket tighter against the winter's cold, to smile at him, to reassure herself that all was well. The pram itself, which Anna's parents had found for him, was like a museum piece – battered, creaky, unsteady on its wheels and now far too small for her rapidly growing brother. Somehow it had survived for over a hundred years to see active service again; somewhere, someone had thought to keep it, just in case. And as it rattled along the pavements, it drew looks from passers-by – looks of surprise, of horror, of confusion. Very occasionally, someone would stop – nearly always a woman, nearly always old, the ones who were alive when Longevity was invented, the ones who remembered what children were like. They would ask to look at 'the baby', their eyes invariably welling up as they told Anna their own story – a lost child, a Declaration signed before the woman understood its true meaning, a longing for something that Anna suspected they dared not articulate, dared not name. But more often, people passing would screw up their faces in looks of disgust; they would gaze haughtily at Anna and Ben as though she were parading something distasteful in public, as though she shouldn't be inflicting his presence on them.

Anna wished she could feel more confident, wished her heart didn't skip a beat every time someone looked at her, every time the computer came on at home, every time the phone rang. She'd longed to leave Grange Hall, had worked hard so that she could become a Valuable Asset and live on the Outside. But increasingly, she was finding it hard to throw off her guilt at being Legal when there were so many Surpluses still incarcerated. Every time someone looked at her, she felt they were judging her. Every time she glimpsed a Surplus working as a house-keeper, imprisoned in the home of their employer, she felt her guilt like a knife-wound deep in her stomach. And they were the lucky ones. They were the ones who were considered Valuable, not simply Useless and Evil.

Doing her best to ignore the stares of the people around her, she walked towards the shopping centre, but as she walked, she saw a large, flickering screen in the window of an electrical store. In front of the window, a small crowd had gathered looking hungrily in at the large, glossy plasma screen. Energy vouchers made such things an unaffordable luxury for most.

Anna, who had grown up without televisions or computers, had never warmed to the disembodied faces and voices that spoke so confidently, peddling their propaganda, telling her what to think about things.

Today, though, she wanted to be brave; instead of walking past, she found herself turning the pram to the right, awkwardly, and joining the throng, easing her way in so that she, too, could watch the silent picture show.

It was a news programme. Anna watched as the camera panned in on a woman talking, then revealed a man being arrested in front of his house. A phone number flashed on the screen with the words 'Energy Watch – report the waste, confidentially assured.' As he was dragged away by the police, Anna felt her insides clench anxiously.

An elderly woman close to Anna shook her head. 'It's like the bloody Cold War again. People snooping on other people. I don't like it. I just don't like it.'

'You may not like it,' another younger-looking woman with artificially auburn hair replied staunchly, 'but if some people abuse the system, there need to be repercussions. I'm sleeping with three blankets and two duvets these days, and then you find out people are tapping into the central grid? I tell you, I'd report them in a flash if I got to hear about it. Wouldn't think twice.'

Anna listened, biting her lip as she watched the screen. She found it hard to judge the world as others seemed able to. Until she'd met Peter, she'd had a very clear idea of what was right and wrong, good and evil, but then her world had been turned upside down, her views challenged, her eyes opened. All those years in Grange Hall she had been told that wrongdoing should be punished, but now, on the Outside, she realised that wrongdoing wasn't always easy to identify, that sometimes the wrong thing was actually the right thing.

The elderly woman turned back to the shop window. 'What's this bloke supposed to have done, anyway?'

'Probably been trading in energy coupons,' a man interjected. 'They're cracking down, aren't they?'

'Trading energy coupons!' The auburn-haired woman tutted. 'As if we don't have enough problems.'

The elderly woman laughed. 'Is that all? Live and let live, that's what I say.'

The auburn-haired woman turned and glared at her. 'Is that all? Sounds like you might be benefiting from illegal coupons,' she said. 'Maybe I'll make a little call to Energy Watch, shall I? Maybe then you won't find it so funny.'

'I was just saying . . .' the elderly woman started to say, but the auburn-haired woman wasn't looking at her any more. Instead, she was looking directly at Anna, who blanched slightly.

'And what have we got here?' Everyone turned and stared at Anna, who now blushed deeply at the attention. 'Only it's not exactly what we need, is it? Here we are struggling to get by, hardworking people just trying to keep warm at night, and we get criminals bringing Surpluses into the world.' She turned back to face Anna. 'Proud of yourself, are you? Oh, I know you got your Legal status, didn't you? Read about it in the papers like everyone else. Bet you know all about playing the system, young lady, don't you? Probably think you're terribly clever. But it's we who suffer. I don't suppose you worry about that, do you?'

'No,' Anna said carefully. 'I don't think I'm clever. But . . .'

'That's probably why I can't get a Surplus house-keeper,' another woman interrupted, ignoring her. 'Making them all Legal, I expect. Four months I've been waiting. Four months and not a word from anyone.'

Anna shook her head. Was that what people really thought? 'No, you're wrong,' she said anxiously. 'They're not making them Legal. They're in Surplus Halls, working day and night to repay their parents' sins. Even though their parents didn't sin. Having children isn't a sin. It isn't . . .'

Her voice trailed off – she knew she'd gone too far, knew that what she'd just said could attract the attention of the police, the Authorities. But then she looked down at Ben who was beginning to stir and felt the familiar feeling of love, of tiger-like protectiveness. How could his existence ever be a sin?

'Isn't a sin?' the auburn-haired woman shrieked, manoeuvring herself so that she blocked Anna's path. 'How dare you? You come here, flaunting that disgusting creature in public; you eat our food, use our energy, and you tell me that you think it's perfectly OK?'

Anna stared at the woman in shock, then she felt her jaw set angrily. 'He isn't disgusting. He's a baby. Surpluses didn't ask to be born. And anyway, I'm Legal now. So's Ben. Our parents died.'

She gripped the pram; her anger made her feel strong, stronger than she'd felt for months.

'Oh, well that's all right then,' the woman said, her voice shaking with emotion. 'Surpluses didn't ask to be born, so it's not their fault. Just like all those immigrants who didn't ask to be smuggled in, I suppose.'

Anna shook her head; the woman's face had gone pink, clashing horribly with her hair.

'They think it's a game, that all they have to do is get to this country and then they can eat our food, live in our houses, use our energy. And where does that leave us? Where does that leave our energy tariffs?'

'I don't know about that,' Anna said evenly. 'You should ask the Authorities.'

'Like they'd do anything,' the woman snorted. 'More border police, that's what they'd say. But it isn't working, is it? They still keep coming, every single day. It's not our fault there are floods. It's not our fault rivers are drying up. I'm sorry, but this is our country and they have to keep these people out.'

'Absolutely,' another voice suddenly said, a soothing, sensible voice. 'I do hope that you get somewhere. You mustn't stop fighting.'

The auburn-haired woman frowned. 'No, I won't,' she said forcefully. 'I've got my rights. We've all got rights and we need to stand up for them, not let these people get away with it. I got a leaflet the other day, pushed through my door, saying we're stealing energy from countries in Africa . . .'

Anna felt a hand on her shoulder. 'Perhaps now might be a good time to go?' the soothing voice said, and Anna looked up to see a kind face framed by grey hair, pulled into a chignon.

'Yes,' she said, pulling the pram back awkwardly. 'Yes, I think you're right.'

She pushed through the crowd, doing her best to avoid sending the wheels over anyone's feet; the grey-haired woman followed her.

'What a lovely little boy he is,' she said, a few moments later. 'How old is he?'

Anna started. No one had ever asked her how old Ben was; it was as if age had ceased to mean anything, even when it could be counted in months.

'He's nearly one,' she said warily.

'What a lovely age. And he's so well behaved.'

'Yes, I suppose he is.' Anna's only knowledge of babies had been gleaned from the Smalls' floor at Grange Hall where the under-fives were left to scream until one of the staff couldn't take the noise any more and reluctantly came to feed or change them. It was partly the memory of those scenes of horror that prompted her to lavish so much attention on Ben, to rush to his side at the first hint of a cry.

'It's Anna, isn't it?' the woman said suddenly. 'You're Anna Covey, aren't you? I wonder, would you like a cup of tea? I only live around the corner. I'm rather an admirer of yours, I must confess. My name is Maria. Maria Whittaker.'

She held out her hand and Anna took it uncertainly.

'No, I don't think so,' she said, biting her lip. 'I should probably get back to my shopping.'

'Of course,' Maria said kindly. 'Then perhaps I could walk with you?'

Anna nodded gratefully. She didn't usually seek company, apart from Peter and Ben's; other people made her feel anxious, on her guard. But this woman seemed so nice, and after the run-in with the horrible auburn-haired lady, she welcomed the companionship. Together they made their way back through the high street, silent at first, until Anna couldn't stop herself from asking the question on the tip of her tongue.

'You . . . you said you were an admirer?' She looked around hesitantly as she spoke, looking out for cameras, for police, for anyone who might be following her. But the street was clear.

The woman laughed. 'I have always admired the young,' she said softly. 'And when I heard your story, well, it touched me. You sounded very brave. You and your friend, Peter. And to look after your brother like that . . . I think it takes a great deal of courage, and, yes, I admire that. I admire it greatly.'

Anna smiled awkwardly. Other than from Peter, she didn't hear kind words very often.

'It wasn't very courageous,' she said quickly. 'Peter was the brave one, not me.'

'I'm sure you were brave too,' Maria said warmly.

Anna found a little smile creeping on to her face. 'You know,' she said, as they turned a corner, 'I might be able to have one cup of tea. If that would be OK.'

Maria returned her smile. 'It would be more than OK. It would be a privilege.'

Maria lived in a modern apartment building just a few minutes' walk from the high street. Her apartment was on the fourth floor, so they left the pram downstairs and Anna carried Ben up the winding staircase.

'I'm so sorry about this. I'm afraid that the lift was decommissioned as part of an energy-saving exercise,' she said, with a rueful smile. 'It's a nightmare with shopping too.'

'Oh, it's no problem,' Anna assured her, pulling Ben to her and holding the banister carefully as she climbed.

'So, do you take sugar?' Maria asked when she'd opened the door to her apartment, revealing a small sitting room with a kitchen area just off it and a narrow corridor which Anna presumed led to the bedroom.

'Yes. Yes, please,' Anna said. 'Just one.'

She followed Maria into the sitting room and stood

next to a sofa as Maria walked over to the small kitchenette in the corner and put on the kettle. On the mantelpiece were photos of children, and Anna stared at them curiously, looking away quickly when Maria handed her a steaming cup of tea and motioned for her to sit on the sofa.

'I'm afraid it isn't very big,' she said, sitting down at the other end. 'My apartment, I mean. But that's the way of things nowadays, isn't it? I used to have a house, you know, years ago, but the rates and energy bills kept increasing and eventually the Authorities encouraged me to move to somewhere smaller.' She smiled wryly.

Anna smiled back. She knew all about how 'encouraging' the Authorities could be. 'It's very nice, though,' she said politely.

'Thank you. I suppose it's comfortable,' Maria said thoughtfully. 'And comfort is, after all, one of the Authorities' prime objectives. Comfort, health, wealth and learning. Worthy goals, I'm sure.'

Anna smiled awkwardly feeling ignorant and hating it. Peter followed every edict and news briefing from the Authorities avidly, using up valuable energy coupons on a computer, switched on daily to check for news and analysis; she couldn't seem to care much about it. So long as she, Peter and Ben were safe and warm, that was all that really mattered. But now, now she wished she'd paid more attention so that she had something to say.

'Of course, you can't be huge fans of the

Authorities,' Maria continued. 'I can't imagine they have many fans amongst the incumbents of Surplus Halls.'

Anna shook her head. The truth was that at Grange Hall the Authorities had been a vague and distant power; the only authority she'd thought about was that of the House Matron.

'It's better now we're out,' she said quietly, hoping that Maria wouldn't notice her sidestepping the question. 'It wasn't very . . . comfortable in Grange Hall.'

Maria smiled ruefully again. 'No, I don't imagine it was. You know, when the Surplus Halls were set up, we were told they would be like schools. Separation from parents was seen as necessary to put people off having them – Surpluses, I mean. And to differentiate them. To make it clear that you . . . that they were different. But they were never meant to be brutal places. And employment – employment was always the end goal, but not slavery. That came later.'

'Later?' Anna asked, curious now. No one ever talked openly about Surpluses, about children, for fear of being labelled a revolutionary, a threat to the Authorities.

'When no one cared any more. People used to, you see. They used to care about civil liberties, about the welfare of Surpluses, about the treatment of illegal immigrants, criminals even. Nowadays, all people care about is how they look, how they feel, how many hours they can have the central heating on, how many hobbies they can take up and discard. They don't like children. They're scared of them. You've seen the way people look at that little man.'

Anna looked down at Ben's chubby face and pulled him closely towards her.

'The photographs,' she said, blushing slightly at the prospect of asking a direct question. 'On your mantelpiece. You're not worried what people might think?'

Maria followed her gaze, her eyes full of pity and sadness.

'Of course. I worry all the time, but that's no reason to hide them away. We can't be scared into doing nothing, Anna, can we?'

Anna shook her head. 'No,' she said. 'But the Authorities . . .'

'The Authorities have too much power,' Maria said immediately. 'Power which they use badly. Power which needs to be challenged.'

Maria moved so that she was sitting close to Anna and took her hand, before looking at her hopefully. 'Anna, I hope you don't mind. These children . . . these photographs . . . they're the reason I invited you here. This one . . .' She walked over and picked up one of the frames, clutching it to her breast before passing it to Anna. 'This one is my child. I was young, foolish, I thought I would manage to keep her secret. But the Catchers . . . well, they found her. Took her away. It was the early days when people were still treated leniently if they apologised; they fined me, but otherwise let me off with a caution because I showed "due remorse". Thought I'd learnt my lesson. But you see, it doesn't work like that, does it?'

Anna quickly took the frame, tears appearing in her eyes as she studied the photograph of a tiny baby, wrapped in a blanket.

'She's a Surplus now?' she asked quietly.

Maria nodded. 'The thing is,' she said, her voice catching slightly, 'at first, when she was taken, I was fine. I had a career, a life to live. I was grateful that I'd avoided a prison sentence; convinced myself it had been a close shave, a lucky break. But as the years went by, I found myself thinking about her. Found myself missing her, desperately, which is silly, because I hardly knew her – just a few weeks, that's all. I found myself seeking out children's things, rummaging through flea markets for vintage items like toys or small blankets. I'd knit little coats for her, sing little nursery rhymes in my head. Even though by that time she'd have been fifty. She'd probably look older than me now. Perhaps she isn't even alive . . .'

Anna saw a tear in Maria's eye as her voice trailed off. She looked back at the photograph and thought of all the Surpluses back at Grange Hall, all the Surpluses around the country.

'Not like you,' Maria continued, appearing to shake herself. 'I suppose you're free to take Longevity now, aren't you?'

Anna shook her head, emboldened by Maria's revelation. 'I'm not . . . I mean, we're not . . . We're going to Opt Out,' she said forcefully. 'We don't want to live for ever.'

Maria nodded, her eyes filled with admiration. 'Of course. You see, I knew that you were courageous. I could see it the first time I saw your photograph in the newspaper. Not like me, Anna. I wasn't courageous; I was weak. I let my daughter down.'

Anna took a sip of tea. 'It wasn't your fault,' she said. It was a line she repeated often, the line she always used when guilty or desperate women accosted her in the street. 'It's not your fault.' 'I'm sure your child was/is happy.' 'I'm sure you'd be a great mother, too.'

'You're kind, Anna, but I'm afraid it is my fault – both the act itself and my inability to get over it. But we find our own ways through times of difficulty, and I've found mine.'

She looked back at the mantelpiece, and Anna followed her gaze, taking in each of the photographs before her.

'Who . . .' she said. 'Who are the other ones?'

'Children like mine,' Maria said simply. 'Babies, toddlers, young children torn away from their mothers. It's too late to track my daughter down. But I try to help others to find their lost children. Talking to anyone who might know something. I thought . . . I thought you might recognise one or two of them. Anything you might be able to do to help . . .'

'They're all Surpluses?' Anna gasped. 'Where did they come from? The photographs, I mean.'

'From their mothers, their fathers, from people who love them,' Maria said softly.

Wedging Ben between two cushions, Anna stood up, steadying herself on the side of the chair as the blood rushed to her head. She walked cautiously towards the mantelpiece, starting at the right end and working her way to the left. To her shock and surprise, she recognised some of them.

'Surplus Sarah,' she said, pulling out a pewter frame cradling a black and white photograph of a young girl. 'She left three years ago. She'll be a housekeeper now. And this one . . .' She pulled out another frame, this one a larger, black frame with a young boy beaming out of it. 'That's Surplus Patrick. He . . .' Anna felt her eyes well up again with anger and indignation as she remembered Surplus Patrick and his constant questions, his insistence that he wasn't a Surplus, that his parents would be coming to find him any day. 'Patrick was sent to a Detention Centre,' she managed to say. 'He didn't fit in very well. He refused to accept that he was a Surplus.'

Maria stood up and took the frame from Anna. 'And you did?'

'I was a Surplus,' Anna said flatly. 'There wasn't anything to accept.'

She returned to the mantelpiece. Face after face, staring out at her hopefully. And then she felt her chest constrict. Right at the far end, was a wooden frame, with a photograph of a toddler. A little girl with faint, red hair and vivid blue eyes.

'Is there another photograph of this girl?' she asked, her heart thudding in her chest. 'One of her a bit older?'

Maria shook her head. 'The parents took it a few years before she was taken away. They didn't take another – taking photographs is a dangerous business, I'm afraid. They count as evidence. Why? You think you know Sheila?'

'Sheila?' Anna gasped, clutching the mantelpiece as a feeling of nausea welled up inside her. 'Sheila was my friend. I left her behind in Grange Hall. I left her behind . . .'

Maria caught her as she fell; she found herself a few moments later back on the sofa, lying down with Maria bending over her, concern in her eyes.

'I . . . I don't know what happened,' she said uneasily. 'I'm sorry. I . . .'

'You fainted,' Maria said gently. 'Are you OK, Anna?'

Anna nodded. 'I'm fine,' she said staunchly. She'd learnt at Grange Hall never to show weakness.

'I'm sure you are. But you must be careful, Anna. Without Longevity your health is weaker than the rest of us. And that little boy is depending on you.'

Anna looked at Ben worriedly, then pulled herself up. 'You've been very kind. But I must go now.'

'Can we see each other again?' Maria asked.

Anna bit her lip, imagining what Peter might say. 'I'm not sure,' she said quietly. Then, her eyes fell back on the photograph of Sheila. 'I mean, maybe,' she corrected herself. 'If I can help.'

Chapter Nine

Peter nearly didn't get to the meeting with Pip on time. Dr Edwards had him studying something called Synthetic PirB all morning and filing the results of a major study in the afternoon, and it had been 5.15 p.m. before he'd been able to get away, and a further twenty minutes before he felt absolutely confident that he wasn't being followed – a regular paranoia that was getting worse lately. As always when meeting Pip, the address wasn't straightforward to find. Number 87 wasn't actually on Grays Inn Road, but round the corner, an old building nestled behind an office block. From the outside it appeared derelict; inside a porter was sitting behind a desk looking half asleep, but he still insisted that Peter sign in before entering. Noticing that he didn't request his identi-card, Peter scribbled the current Underground password; the guard nodded and Peter headed for the stairs.

He needn't have rushed, in the event; Pip was ten minutes late. The room was small, grey, with a meeting table in the middle and a haphazard arrangement of cheap metal chairs around it. Peter pulled one out and sat on it, then looked around. There was little to hold his attention; the walls were covered in peeling, colourless wallpaper, and a whiteboard hung listlessly from one wall. There were no blinds at the window, but none were necessary because of the accumulated grease and dirt which prevented anyone from seeing in – or out.

'This place is being turned into flats next month,' Peter heard Pip's familiar voice say, and he turned round quickly. Pip never announced his presence; he always seemed to appear from nowhere, skulking into rooms unnoticed, his blue eyes twinkling at people's surprise.

'Flats are more energy efficient,' Peter replied.

The answer appeared to satisfy Pip. 'So, how's Pincent Pharma?'

Peter shrugged. 'Fine. I'm kind of getting the hang of it. So haven't you found a new headquarters yet?'

Pip didn't appear to notice the question. 'And your grandfather. Have you seen much of him?'

Peter bristled as he thought of their conversation the day before. 'A bit. He keeps telling me how great Longevity is. Trying to convince me not to Opt Out.'

'You told him you were Opting Out?' Pip's voice was incredulous. 'You just told him?'

Peter faltered slightly. 'You said to be as honest as possible. And I only said I hadn't decided yet.'

'I said not to tell too many lies because you'd get confused. I also told you to tell him you were planning to sign . . . Oh, Peter.' He shook his head, and Peter found his chest tensing uncomfortably.

'It just came out,' he said. 'But it's OK, honestly. Don't you trust me?'

'Of course I trust you,' Pip said, but his eyes were still worried. They made Peter feel guilty; the guilt made him irritable.

'No, you don't. You think I'm just a kid. You think I don't know anything. But I do. I know what I'm doing.'

Pip nodded, then looked at the grimy window. 'I know you do, Peter. But you don't know how persuasive your grandfather can be. I do.'

'He's not *persuasive*,' Peter said, his defences rising further. 'I think he talks total rubbish. He thinks young people are a waste of space.'

'And a threat to him.' Pip allowed himself a little smile. 'You know, Peter, a few hundred years ago, many countries in the world considered slavery to be a perfectly sound way to run businesses and households. A bit like the attitude to Surpluses now. Most people didn't have the vote and women were considered the property of their husbands.'

Peter looked down. 'Do I have "please give me a history lesson" written on my forehead?' he muttered. 'Because you're the second person to give me one in as many days.'

Pip raised an eyebrow. 'Many people lost their lives fighting for these rights – to vote, to be free, to work, to be able to get on the same bus as someone considered their superior. And it was the next generations who embedded these changes, who came to view women as equals to men, who came to understand that skin colour is of no relevance. Young people are the future. Without them, the world stands still.'

'I know that,' Peter said, a little too quickly.

'Good,' Pip said seriously. 'Because people like your grandfather don't see it like that. They think that youth can be dispensed with, that the world won't suffer.'

'I know.' Peter looked down, trying to push the image of Anna dying, in need of Longevity drugs, from his head. 'I know Longevity is wrong. Unlike Dr Edwards. He thinks it's beautiful.'

'Dr Edwards?'

Peter nodded. 'He's the one who's been teaching me. I work in his lab.'

'You're in Dr Edwards' lab?' Pip, for once, looked slightly shaken.

'Do you know him? He's Head of ReTraining.'

'ReTraining.' Pip frowned, then nodded. 'You know, Dr Edwards used to be one of Pincent's most powerful scientists. Be very careful, Peter. Dr Edwards is dangerous.'

'Dangerous? Dr Edwards? He couldn't scare a crow,' Peter said incredulously.

'Danger manifests itself in many ways, Peter. Brilliance of mind can be as dangerous as a loaded weapon.'

'Well, you're wrong,' Peter said. 'Dr Edwards isn't dangerous. He's all right, actually. He's just a science geek. And he said he likes young people because he likes being contradicted.'

Pip didn't say anything for a few seconds, and Peter found himself reddening slightly – he'd never told Pip he was wrong about anything before. He looked up tentatively, to see Pip's reaction.

'A science geek,' Pip said, his tone more insistent than before. 'Yes, I suppose you're right. But you see, Peter, the trouble with science geeks, as you call them, is that they put discovery before anything else. It was a science geek who discovered the atom bomb. He didn't intend to cause mass murder, but he did nonetheless. Believe me when I say that you can't trust Dr Edwards. You can't trust anyone.'

'Except you, you mean?' Peter asked, raising his eyebrows. Then he shrugged, shot Pip a sheepish smile. 'Look, I am careful. And honestly, I can handle Dr Edwards. He's OK.'

'OK?' Pip's voice was still insistent. 'Peter, Dr Edwards is not on our side. Those not for us are against us, are a danger to us.'

Peter felt himself getting impatient. 'You always say that. But it isn't true,' he said, irritation creeping into his voice. 'Just because someone isn't in the Underground, doesn't make them evil. Things aren't always black and white, you know.' His flush deepened as he realised he was repeating his grandfather's words, and he crossed his arms defensively.

Pip didn't say anything. Then he nodded, his eyes full of concern, and put his hand on Peter's shoulder. 'If I'm overprotective, Peter, it's because you are so important to us. You and Anna represent the new beginning, our hope for the future.' He looked intently at Peter; Peter found he couldn't see anything but Pip's eyes boring into his. 'You represent so much to the Underground, Peter,' he said softly. 'And so much to me personally. I have seen you grow from a child; soon you will be a man. I only wish to guide you, to point out the dangers. That's all.'

Peter's eyes moved downwards. 'I know. Look, I'll be careful,' he said quietly.

'I know you will. I'll make contact soon,' Pip said, walking towards the door, and then he was gone.

Chapter Ten

Anna was at the stove when Peter got back that evening, and when he saw her earnest expression, the lines of concentration etched into her forehead, it reminded him of the first time he'd seen her, staring up at a Grange Hall instructor, desperate to please, to Get Things Right. She turned when she heard him come in, her face immediately easing into a smile, and Peter rushed over to pick her up in his arms, before lifting up Ben and holding him aloft. Ben's skin was impossibly soft and he immediately broke out in giggles as Peter nuzzled his tummy with his nose. He wished Dr Edwards could see this; to see why really being young was so much better than Renewal. No drugs or synthetic proteins could create the youthful excitement and abandonment that came so naturally to Ben.

'So how was your day?' Anna asked, stirring what looked like soup.

Peter shrugged and put Ben down. 'It was good,' he said noncommittally.

'You saw Pip?' Anna mouthed the words and Peter nodded.

'And?'

'Nothing,' he mouthed back. 'Nothing new.'

Anna nodded. 'No, come here. Oh, you naughty boy.' Ben was crawling towards the kitchen door and Anna left the stove to chase after him, scooping him up. 'He needs more space to move around,' she sighed, as she returned to her cooking. 'I wish we had a bigger garden.'

Peter grinned. 'Say it a bit louder and they might hear you,' he said mischievously, then leant down so his head was nearer hers. He breathed in the smell of her hair, felt the thrill that always shot through him when he was close to her.

Ben cried and Anna pulled away to pick him up. He had crawled under a chair, knocking it over in the process and was now trapped with the chair on its side.

'Oh, Ben, oh little man. Oh, come here. It's OK. It's OK,' she soothed. 'He's been grizzly all day. I think maybe he's tired.'

'You think you should put him down to sleep?' Peter asked.

Anna shook her head. 'If he goes down now, he'll be awake at the crack of dawn. I'd rather wait. And he hasn't eaten yet.'

Peter picked up the chair and sat down on it heavily, his eyes resting on the gnarled wood of the kitchen table in front of him, the marks and knots that had appeared as the tree it was made from had grown. The table was old, inherited from Anna's parents. It was made from oak, a solid thing. Oak trees lived for hundreds of years, he found himself thinking. That wasn't wrong. It was natural. Were there different rules for different species?

'I think maybe Ben's hungry. I might give him a little snack before we eat. Can you turn off the stove?'

Peter stood up and flicked the switch absently.

'There we go. Lovely yogurt,' he heard Anna say. Then she lowered her voice. 'So what did Pip say?'

Peter shrugged, trying not to resent the fact that he never seemed to get her full attention these days. 'Oh, nothing really,' he mouthed dismissively. 'Don't worry about it. So, any post today?'

Anna pointed to a pile on the table; a pile she'd left untouched, her mind preoccupied with other things, with Maria, with the Surpluses up and down the country. Peter rummaged through it, discarding half of the letters as junk without opening them. Then he started slightly.

'We got these today?' he asked, picking out two large envelopes with the distinctive logo of the Authorities stamped across them. Anna's eyes widened; she hadn't even noticed them.

Peter took his and turned it over in his hands. 'Are you thinking what I'm thinking?'

Anna said nothing, but the look in her eyes suggested that she was. Slowly, Peter slipped his thumb under the flap, ripped the envelope open and pulled out the letter.

'Dear Peter,
As you are approaching your sixteenth birthday,
I am delighted to enclose the Declaration for you
to sign. As you will know, signing the
Declaration entitles you to take Longevity™,
prolonging your life indefinitely.

The Declaration is an important document,
and I hope you will take the time to read it
carefully. Longevity™ has changed the world for
humans, allowing us the freedom of limitless time
and limitless health. It is a truly wondrous thing,
but there is a cost to be born . . .'

Peter felt the hairs on the back of his neck stand on end. This was it. This was the letter.

He scanned it quickly, taking in only snatches. '*. . . by signing the Declaration, and thereby benefiting from a prolonged, healthful life, you agree to take all necessary precautions to ensure that you do not bring any Surplus life into the world . . . Should you discover your responsibility only when a Surplus life is born into the world, it is imperative that you contact the Authorities . . . cooperation will reduce any sentence imposed . . .*'

It was signed by the Secretary General of the Authorities. But the letter was of less interest to Peter than the document with it. He handed the letter to Anna, who read it, her eyes widening as she did so before she handed it back to him. Then, slowly, deliberately, Peter turned to the document itself. Across the top was written: *The Declaration*. He'd heard so much about the Declaration, blamed it for so much that was wrong with the world. And now, his own was in his hands. Feeling his heart quicken, Peter began to read.

When in the course of scientific development and progress it became clear that the function and roles of humans had changed fundamentally, that the basic tenets of procreation for survival had been challenged and found wanting, it became compelling for humankind to respond to this development and progress.

Man has for many thousands of years relied on Nature to increase their numbers and has, at the same time, been in thrall to Nature and Her whims, including disease, pestilence, famine and other plagues that have culled great numbers of humans.

The cycle of birth, life and death has resulted in other burdens, reducing humankind to the enslaved position of animals, with no control over their future. Indeed, so used to slavery was Man that he created masters to worship and follow, gods who imposed rules and laws that contradict and contravene Man's true nature.

It is in science that Man has finally surpassed Nature; through science, Man has developed Longevity™, the most significant discovery of Man's time on earth. Longevity™ enables humankind to live as gods, to live freely, unencumbered by the ravages that Nature imposes on them. Longevity™, through the process of Renewal™, has brought about a New Age for Man, an age of comfort, joy, prosperity and learning. An Age of Freedom.

Freedom, however, brings with it responsibilities: responsibilities to the planet, to our fellow man, and to Nature Herself. Therefore, as a responsible citizen of the United Kingdom, under the governance of the Authorities of the United Kingdom, I, the undersigned, do solemnly Declare, that I will take every measure and precaution to ensure that I will never be responsible for the creation of new human life (forthwith to be referred to as Surplus), accepting any method deemed appropriate by the Authorities and allowing their appointed doctors to insert implants or other methods as appropriate, and that if I should break this Declaration either through intent or by error, or discover that a fellow subject has broken the Declaration on my behalf, that I will contact the appropriate Authorities forthwith and submit myself and any other parties to the action determined by these Authorities, in the full knowledge that the balance of Nature must be maintained, that A Life for a Life is enshrined in law and in everything that is moral and right.

Accepting this, and confirming that I gratefully

*accept the indefinite life that Longevity™ will
provide me, I do hereby solemnly swear.*

Signed: *Witness:*   *Date:*

He put it down. A light veil of sweat coated his forehead; his hands were shaking slightly.

'They don't even mention the Opt Out clause,' he
said. He had intended his voice to appear light, confident, as though receiving his Declaration didn't faze
him in the slightest, but his throat caught, making
him sound strangled, tense. 'So are you going to open
yours?'

Anna shook her head, her lips pursed together.
'Why should I?' she said. 'I'm not interested in the
Declaration.'

Peter frowned. 'You're not even curious?'

'No. I'm not signing, so why should I even look at
it?'

'Just because I want to read my Declaration doesn't
mean I'm thinking about signing it.' The words left
Peter's mouth before he'd had time to consider them,
to realise how defensive, how aggressive they
sounded.

Anna looked at him incredulously. 'Of course I
know that. Why would you even say that?'

'Pip thinks I might.' He hadn't realised how much
Pip's doubt had got to him, how much it had unsettled him.

'He can't do. Why would he?' Anna's eyebrows

were raised, a look of utter disbelief on her face. She trusted him completely, Peter realised. It wouldn't cross her mind that he might be tempted to sign.

He shrugged. 'How should I know? Maybe he's worried about the Pincent blood in my veins. Maybe he thinks I'm too young to know what I want.'

Anna moved towards him, put her arms around his neck. 'Don't listen to him. You'd never sign the Declaration,' she whispered forcefully. 'I know you wouldn't.'

Peter turned his head and looked at her for a moment, remembering how convinced she'd been when he first met her that Surpluses were a Burden on Mother Nature, that it was their duty to work hard, to serve Legal people, to pay for their Sin of existence. He pulled her head down and kissed the top of it. 'Of course I wouldn't,' he mouthed, stroking her hair. 'We'll grow old and wrinkly and have children. And we'll put an end to Longevity too, I promise.'

Chapter Eleven

Jude lay in bed, frown lines etched into his forehead. The Underground hadn't contacted him again, and it was eating at him. He'd convinced himself that their little visit had been part of an initiation process, that he'd simply had to prove himself, that any day now they'd contact him again, tell him how he could help. So he'd waited for them, staring at his computer screen willing it to show a message from them, taken his mini-com with him everywhere just in case he was out when they got in touch. But it was all for nothing. There were no signals, no suggestion that he had made any impact on them at all. Peter Pincent they helped; Peter Pincent they cared about enough to get out of Grange Hall. Jude, on the other hand – who had real skills that might be useful to them – they weren't interested in. No wonder his dad had said the Underground were a bunch of losers.

Doing his best to swallow his disappointment, Jude got up and turned on his computer. It was 11 a.m. – time to start the day. He didn't care about the Underground, he told himself. He didn't need them.

Until recently, he had barely registered their existence. Until recently, he hadn't even known about Peter, about having a half-brother. And he was happy to forget all about them both. More than happy.

Without thinking, he sat back low in his chair, hacked into the Pincent Pharma security system and brought up an image of Pincent Pharma on his screen. So much for Peter's gratitude towards the Underground – now he was working for their sworn enemy, Pincent Pharma. Served them right, Jude thought to himself. They should pick their friends more carefully.

He stared at the screen and imagined Peter inside, wondered what he was doing. Sometimes he hated him. Poor old unlucky Peter Pincent whose legality had been snatched away from him, who had grown up with nothing, who had been brave and fearless, who newspapers seemed obsessed with. Like he was dangerous or something. Like he had some hidden powers. He was a Surplus, that was all. If he'd been born just a couple of months earlier . . . well, things would have been different. Very different. Legal status wasn't all it was cracked up to be in Jude's opinion. Peter should try growing up with a father who resented him and a mother who only had you to get one over her lover's wife. Then he'd know what 'unlucky' really meant.

Pushing the thought from his mind, he turned back to the screen. Across the front of the building, the words 'Pincent Pharma' blazed out, making Jude shift uncomfortably. Pincent. The Pincents. It was a name that carried such weight, that everyone in the world knew. Pincent Pharma, the most powerful company. And now there was Peter Pincent, the Surplus who escaped.

Curious suddenly, Jude delved further into the security system, looking for more images, surveillance of the inside of the building. Perhaps he'd see Peter walking along a corridor, or working, doing whatever it was he did in there. Jude couldn't see the appeal of a job like that, working inside a rabbit warren with cameras everywhere. Actually, Jude couldn't really see the appeal of a job full stop – having to get up every morning and do as someone else told you. The whole point of being grown-up, in Jude's opinion, was doing what you wanted.

Quickly, he brought up more images, trying to track Peter down. But it was pointless – there were as many cameras in Pincent Pharma as there were Authorities' edicts on energy consumption and Jude figured it would take hours to look at them all. Sighing, he decided to give up. But as he moved his mouse to close the window, he frowned. On his screen was the image of a girl. About his age, maybe a bit younger. Jude hadn't seen an actual girl for . . . well, ever, actually, apart from the odd photograph of a Surplus in the newspaper, or a little glimpse of a Surplus housekeeper through someone's window. Jude couldn't afford a housekeeper himself, although he'd been tempted to make some more money so he could, just to see what it would be like to have someone his own age to talk to.

He stared at the screen. The girl was red-haired and was lying on a bed, her face pale, her eyes closed. Was she sleeping? Why? And what was she doing at Pincent Pharma? All these questions flashed through Jude's head at once, but he couldn't begin to answer them; all he could do was look, in wonder, in amazement, in . . . in hope, he realised. Hope that she might open her eyes. That she might look into the camera, meet his eyes. It was impossible, of course, Jude knew that; she wouldn't meet his eyes or have any inkling that he even existed. But still, he hoped that she'd wake up.

His eyes flicked around the screen – at the bottom was the code for her whereabouts: Unit X. Then, suddenly, as his eyes returned to her face, he felt something clenching inside him. Her eyes opened, but they weren't at peace; they were filled with terror. Of what, Jude couldn't see, but he felt it; deep down in the pit of his stomach he felt her desperation. Then, suddenly, the picture was replaced by another image, a corridor, along which guards were patrolling.

'No!' Jude shouted, immediately bringing up the camera control function, jabbing at his keyboard to get the girl back. But he couldn't find her. Frustratedly, he searched the security system, flicked from camera to camera, but to no avail. It was as though he'd imagined her. As though she didn't exist. Except he knew she did. And he also knew that he couldn't leave her there, not like that, not with agony etched into her eyes.

He thought for a minute, then, carefully navigated out of the security system and brought up a new page, scrolling down it until he had the information he needed. Then, he picked up his phone and dialled a number.

'Welcome to Pincent Pharma. Please press 1 to be put through to our twenty-four hour helpline, 2 for our latest product information, 3 for dosage information, 4 for advice on ageing . . .'

Jude pressed the hash key, followed by 349.

'This is Richard Pincent. Please leave a message.'

Feeling his heart quicken, Jude cleared his throat. 'This message concerns Pincent Pharma security and information regarding the recent Underground attacks. I am a friend; I can help. If you're interested, please leave me a message at www.LogBook.290.' Then, ignoring his shaking hands and the feeling of trepidation in his stomach, he turned off his computer and went downstairs to make some coffee.

Peter only found the note in his coat pocket as he arrived at work; he didn't know whether it had been put there the night before or that morning on his way to work. It didn't matter either way; what mattered was that he had his first proper mission. Printed in small, neat lettering, in the familiar Underground typography and layout, were the words 'We need file 23b from RP's office. Pls secure. Destroy this note.'

Peter memorised the file number and thrust the note back in his pocket, burning it as soon as he got to the lab. It was more direct than anything he'd ever received from the Underground, he realised as he watched it being eaten by the hungry flame. Perhaps Pip was beginning to really trust him. Maybe he was finally seeing him as a man, not a boy.

'Peter. A word?'

It was his grandfather. Peter started, blew the ash in front of him off the counter, hardly dared to think what would have happened if he'd appeared seconds earlier. 'Sure,' he said casually, as he felt the muscles on the back of his neck tighten.

They walked down the corridor towards the lift, then travelled in silence, as before, to Richard's large office. Several guards were positioned outside, their beady eyes sweeping the corridor for anyone who shouldn't be there. To the side of the door was a key-pad into which his grandfather entered an eight-digit number; Peter watched carefully, whilst appearing to check his watch for the time. Once inside, Peter was ushered into a comfortable chair opposite his grandfather's desk.

'So,' his grandfather said, sitting down behind his desk and offering him a cup of coffee. 'I just wondered how your deliberations were going.'

'Deliberations?'

'To sign, or not to sign.' Peter noticed his grandfather's left hand tapping nervously, the slight twitch in his right eye, the colour of his face – more grey than it had been the week before.

Peter looked around the room, scanning it for files. 'I haven't really thought about it,' he said cautiously, taking a gulp of coffee.

His grandfather put his cup down. The motion was heavy, causing a clank as the porcelain hit the table. Then he pushed back his chair, picking up a file in front of him and flicking through it idly; Peter could tell from the way his eyes were moving that they weren't focusing on it. He wondered which file it was. Wondered how easy the filing system was to work out.

The phone rang, and his grandfather picked it up. 'I see,' he said, after several seconds. 'Very well.' He put the phone down, then lifted it again and pressed a button. 'Yes, I'd like to order a car . . . This evening, 5 p.m. To the West End. Thank you.' He put the receiver down, then his eyes fell on Peter, as though surprised to find him still there. 'Ah, Peter,' he said vaguely. 'I'm sorry about that. Where were we?'

Peter looked at him archly. 'You were asking me if I'd decided to sign the Declaration.'

'That's right.' He continued to look at Peter, his expression unreadable. Peter was tempted to get up and walk out, but he didn't.

'That's it?' he asked instead. 'That's all you wanted to say?'

His grandfather smiled, then stood up. 'Not signing would be a huge mistake,' he said thoughtfully, as he walked around to the front of his desk and leant against it. 'You know that.'

'To be honest, I haven't really had time to think properly.' Peter's eyes followed his grandfather like a hawk.

'So then there is nothing else to say,' Richard said smoothly.

This time, Peter didn't say anything; he just got up to go.

'You know, you and I are alike, Peter,' his grandfather continued; reluctantly, Peter sat down again. 'I can see it in your eyes. We both want to achieve great things, to be someone. Perhaps you think that Opting Out would mark you out from the crowd, make you different, unique. But if you Opt Out, you won't be making a statement; you'll be signing your life away, quite literally.'

'We're not alike.' The words burst out before Peter could stop himself; immediately his grandfather smiled broadly.

'Oh yes we are. We both enjoy a fight. Both enjoy winning. Both like to have the last word, isn't that right?'

Peter's eyes narrowed.

'Tell me, Peter, how many members of the Underground have Opted Out?' his grandfather asked, ignoring Peter's silence. 'How many of them were prepared to make the sacrifice that you are being asked to?'

Peter shrugged. 'How would I know? I don't know anyone from the Underground.'

'Of course you don't,' his grandfather said smoothly. 'Foolish of me.' He smiled. 'You know, in the past terrorists used to convince passionate young men to blow themselves up for some cause or other all the time. Revolutionaries are always keen to find sacrificial lambs. So long as they don't have to die themselves.'

'I wouldn't know about that.'

'No, I'm sure you don't. Just remember, Peter, that indecisiveness is a very poor quality. People need to know where you stand. *I* need to know where you stand.'

Peter stood up again. 'Look, I can't rush a decision like this,' he said, doing his best to give nothing away in his voice.

His grandfather looked him directly in the eye for a second, then nodded. 'Of course. Of course you can't.'

Peter turned and made his way back to the door.

'Oh, and Peter,' his grandfather said, as he opened it.

'What?'

'You very nearly got the last word. Well done.'

Peter opened his mouth to speak, then, irritably, forced it closed and walked out of the door.

Chapter Twelve

'Right, I think we're done for the day. You ready to go home?'

Peter shook his head distractedly as though embroiled in the experiment Dr Edwards had asked him to complete. 'Me? No. I wanted to . . . finish up a few things.'

'OK, suit yourself.'

From his position at the side of the room, Peter waited impatiently as Dr Edwards walked around the lab, turning things off, checking machines, flicking alarms, until finally he waved goodbye and left. Then Peter waited, even more impatiently, for fifteen minutes to pass – just in case Dr Edwards came back, just in case he was right outside the laboratory talking to someone. And then, finally, he put his own coat on, and slipped out of the door into the empty corridor. With his own ears he'd heard his grandfather order a car – right now, he would be speeding towards the West End through empty streets. This was Peter's best chance to get the file. Possibly his only chance.

Quickly, he made his way down the brightly lit

white corridors, his eyes drawn as he walked to their high ceilings, the bright posters of cells that hung on the walls. Everywhere he looked was bright, white, enticing, like everywhere else within Pincent Pharma's four walls. It was hard to imagine that anything bad could be created in such a clean and pure environment.

Finally, Peter arrived at the lifts and, seeing a door to the left, opened it. As he expected, there were stairs leading up and down – a safer option, he decided, bounding up two steps at a time. Checking he was on the right floor, he opened the door ahead of him cautiously. This corridor was empty too, large and bright like all the others, but unlike the corridor outside the training lab, this corridor, Peter knew, was patrolled by guards. Slowly but surely, his eyes and ears alert to the smallest movement, he made his way towards his grandfather's office, all the way practising in his head his excuse if he were caught: *I wanted to talk to my grandfather. I was having doubts about Opting Out. I thought I might have left something behind when I was in the office earlier*. He still didn't know exactly how he would get past the guards, but he had convinced himself that he'd find a way – they would change shifts at one point, they would become distracted, take a coffee break. If he waited long enough, his chance would come. It had to.

To his surprise, though, when he turned the corner, he discovered that the guards who patrolled the corridors outside his grandfather's office weren't there.

The cameras were still operating, but watching them for a short while, Peter realised that for a full thirty seconds every few minutes, they were all facing away from the door.

Not quite believing his good fortune, and timing his movements to perfection, Peter waited for them to move then sprung silently towards the door, his heart beating fast in his chest. Quietly, he knocked, then more loudly. Looking around, cautiously, he turned to the security key pad and entered the eight-digit number he'd memorised earlier that day. The door swung open immediately and he slipped inside, looking around furtively for any sign of the room being occupied, but it was empty. The lights were on, but his grandfather was nowhere to be seen; a half-drunk cup of coffee on the desk was cold, suggesting that no one had been in this room for at least an hour.

Peter's eyes quickly scanned the room, plotting a way forward, formulating a plan. There were cupboards, filing cabinets, shelves, any of which could contain the file he was looking for, along with a computer on his grandfather's desk, which for all Peter knew could hold the key to Longevity itself. He wanted to search everything comprehensively, but he knew it was impossible – he didn't have the time, couldn't risk disturbing anything. Even without cameras, this room would have its own security measures; measures Peter couldn't even see.

He would find the file and he would go. Immediately.

But as he approached the desk, he found himself drawn to his grandfather's chair. It was a large brown leather chair that swung from side to side and rolled across the floor easily; as Peter lowered himself into it, he realised that it could spin a full circle. Allowing himself to relax, he sank further into the leather. It was indecently comfortable – large, soft, solid. In it, Peter felt weighty, significant. This was not a chair for the faint-hearted; it was a chair of power.

Slowly, deliberately, he rolled himself towards his grandfather's desk, the large imposing mahogany table that he'd only ever seen the other side of. It was huge – at least three metres long and two wide – on large legs with ornate carvings. The bulk of the top was covered in dark red leather, embossed with gold round the edge. And right in the middle of the leather was a file 'Chemical Components and Supply'. Peter opened it quickly, his eyes scanning the contents. It was meaningless to him, just a list of abbreviations and companies.

Then, shaking himself, he stood up and walked over to the shelves at the side of the office. Tall leather boxes lined the shelves, each numbered: 1–3a; 4–7a; 8–10a. Scanning downwards, Peter soon found the b's; moments later he was pulling out 23b. It was entitled 'Pincent Pharma Terminology and Abbreviations'. Immediately Peter tucked it in the waistband of his trousers under his shirt.

Then, looking around furtively, he frowned. He'd done it, he realised suddenly. He'd got the file. And it had been easy.

Quickly, he returned to the desk, moved everything back to exactly where it had been when he walked in. But as he did so, his eye caught something, some words, typed on to white paper, lodged between other papers in a tray on the left of the desk. One word in particular stood out: 'Surplus'.

Bristling slightly – the very term 'Surplus' was a constant source of anger and disgust to Peter – he carefully pulled the page out; with it came twenty or so more pages which were stapled to it. The front page, the one that Peter's eyes had alighted upon, had just one line of type on it, all capital letters: 'SURPLUS MANAGEMENT PROGRAMME'. Below this, scribbled in pencil was a note: 'Richard, have you seen this? I think you need to . . .'

Frowning, Peter turned the page and started to read. It was a fairly dull, if utterly offensive, review of the measures that were being used to 'manage' the Surplus Problem. It outlined the use of Surplus Halls, the role of the Surplus Police or 'Catchers', the education programme to encourage citizens to report any sight or sound of babies or children. It contained spreadsheets identifying the cost-per-Surplus, and analysing ways to bring this cost down, and a paper discussing the colour of overalls and whether grey might be a more suitable colour for them than navy – less cheerful, less easy to soil. Peter flicked the pages over angrily, his mouth curled up in distaste. And then he came to a page entitled 'Surplus Sterilisation

Programme'. His brow furrowing further, Peter began to read.

'. . . As agreed by clause 54.67d of the 2124 Surplus Bill . . . would initiate a programme of irreversible sterilisation of all Surplus children on arrival at a Surplus Hall . . . inhibit further Surplus production . . . as part of routine medical . . . Successful trial revealed few problems . . . less aggression in male Surpluses owing to lower testosterone levels and no obvious effects seen in females . . .'

Peter stared at the page, the words beginning to swim before his eyes as they sank in, drowning him, pulling him into deep, angry water. Irreversible sterilisation? Was he reading what he thought he was reading? Slowly, he turned the page, to see a list of names. There were hundreds of them, all with dates next to them, and their location and age. He could barely bring himself to look. But he had to, flicking desperately through the pages until he found what he was looking for, what he'd hoped he wouldn't find, and when he did he felt his heart crash into his feet and the blood drain from his face. It was there in black and white: 'Surplus Anna (F), 2127 (2), Grange Hall (South)'. Frantically he turned the pages, searching for his own name; finally, he found it, towards the end. 'Surplus Peter (M), 2140 (15) Grange Hall (South)*.'

He had to turn two more pages to find the definition of the asterisk: 'Late Entrant'. All at once images flooded into his brain – of the injections he'd been given at Grange Hall; of Pip telling him it was his responsibility to bring new life into the world; of the Declarations he and Anna so nearly Opted Out of, for nothing.

He leant against the desk to steady himself. The walls seemed as though they were caving in on him; in front of him he could see only darkness. There would be no new generation. He wasn't the Underground's greatest hope. Pulling himself up, Peter looked around the room wildly, then, only just remembering to scan the corridor for guards and wait for the cameras, he ran from the room.

Chapter Thirteen

Peter didn't go home immediately. He couldn't face Anna, couldn't face telling her what he'd just learnt, not when it was so new to him, not when he hadn't been able to process the information, or even to establish how to react. So, instead, he walked the streets of South London; found a bar that allowed its customers to bypass its identi-card scanner and bought a drink – a vodka and orange juice – then another one. The bar was full – evidently, Peter wasn't the only person who had had his fill of life that day. Old-looking men and women sat hunched over tables, nursing drinks, muttering to each other, to themselves.

The barman looked at him curiously, but didn't say anything. He simply took Peter's money and gave him his drink. Peter downed it straight away and ordered another.

'Drinking a bit quickly, aren't you?'

Peter turned to see that a man had joined him at the bar. His face was red, bloated; his eyes bulged out of their sockets as though straining to be free.

'What's it to you?' Peter emptied the glass into his mouth and ordered another. Yet another adult telling him what to do. Yet another adult thinking he knew better, thinking he knew it all.

'Nothing, I s'pose. What you drinking anyway?'

Peter looked at him for a moment, then shrugged. 'Vodka,' he said.

The man peered at him. 'How old are you?'

Peter took a gulp of his drink, ignoring the man, who was getting on his nerves. He wanted to be left alone to think, to brood, to tame the anger welling up inside him, to turn it into something manageable. But instead of allowing him to drink in peace, the man repeated his question, forcing Peter to turn back to him. 'Does it matter?' he asked tightly.

The man thought for a moment, then shook his head. 'Nah. Don't suppose it does.'

He appeared to lose interest in Peter then; Peter took another gulp of his drink, then stared down into it. In the reflection in the glass he could see his face, distorted, twisted, like a strange freak of nature, like an idiot. Had he been an idiot? Did the Underground know about the sterilisation programme? No, they couldn't. They just couldn't. Pip wouldn't have been so keen for Peter to Opt Out if he knew there was no point. If he couldn't have children anyway.

'Haven't seen you in here before, have I?'

Reluctantly, Peter turned back to the man still standing next to him. 'I'm sorry?' His tone wasn't so irritable this time. The alcohol was warming his stomach, making his head fuzzy.

'Haven't seen you before,' the man repeated.

'No,' Peter said vaguely. 'No, you haven't.'

His grandfather had said that the Underground wanted him to throw his life away for their cause. Was he right? Why hadn't Pip Opted Out? Why was it one rule for him and another for his followers?

'I thought as much,' the man said, nodding seriously. 'I don't remember seeing you before and my memory isn't too bad. Not usually.'

'Right,' Peter said. He felt angry with Pip suddenly. He should have known about the Surplus Sterilisation Programme. He should have told him.

The man grimaced. 'How old did you say you were?' he asked.

'I didn't,' Peter said. 'Is it really so important?'

The man shook his head. 'Not usually. Not for most folks. You, though, you're different, aren't you? You're that Surplus that was in the papers.'

Peter sighed. 'So then you know how old I am,' he said.

'Hmmm,' the man said, nodding slowly to himself. 'So young. So new.' He put his hand on Peter's. 'You wait a few years, then you'll see,' he said lugubriously.

'Thanks,' Peter said tightly. 'Thanks for the tip.' He drained his glass, looked at his watch, thought about Anna, thought about leaving. Then he shrugged and ordered another. What did it matter anyway? What did anything matter now?

The man laughed. 'You're welcome,' he said, pretending to doff his cap. 'You're welcome, I'm sure.'

Peter opened his mouth to say something, then closed it again. Pip wanted him and Anna to Opt Out. To cut their lives short – for what? To make a point? Was that all his life was worth in Pip's opinion? Angrily, he slammed his glass down on the counter. Pip had betrayed him; the Underground had. And they'd betrayed Anna too. They'd pretended to care, and all the time . . .

'I wouldn't worry about it,' the man next to him said conversationally. 'Whatever it is you're vexed about, can't be that bad.'

'Can't it?' Peter swung round and stared at the man. He could feel himself sway, noticed that his words were slurring slightly. 'And you'd know, would you?'

The man smiled and shrugged. 'Nothing matters, you see. What goes around comes around and what doesn't come around . . . well, that goes around too.'

'You're wrong,' Peter said, his voice low and angry. 'Everything matters. I matter. Anna matters. Our lives matter.'

'If you say so,' the man said.

'I do say so,' Peter said forcefully, almost forgetting that he was talking to a stranger. 'If you think nothing matters, then it's OK to use people. And it's OK to believe in people who let you down. But it isn't.' He rocked forward slightly and pulled himself back just in time to avoid falling off the stool.

'They let you down, you let them down, then

they're your best friend, until next time,' the man said, the words almost sounding poetic as they came out of his mouth, like a rhyme, or a folk song. He looked at Peter for a few seconds, then he shrugged. 'It all just goes round and round, you see,' he muttered. 'You'll find out. Can't make a bad choice, can't make a good one.'

'You're talking rubbish,' Peter said, abruptly pulling himself upright and starting when the room began to spin violently. 'Of course you can make a bad choice. You can choose to trust the wrong people. You can choose to believe them . . .' he trailed off, fighting the tears that were pricking at his eyes.

The man leant closer and Peter gagged slightly at the smell of alcohol on his breath.

'Trust who you want. Right and wrong, they're just the same.' He stared at Peter, his bulbous eyes focused on Peter's with an intensity that made him uncomfortable, then he erupted into rasping laughter. 'So, you going to make better choices? That why you're in here?'

Peter pulled himself off the stool and put some money down on the counter. 'I don't know,' he said quietly, swaying, his vision now blurred, his heart heavy in his chest. 'I don't know what the right choice is. I don't know if I even have one any more.'

'None of us does,' the man said sagely, downing his drink. 'We thinks we do, but we don't. Not really. Best thing to do is just sit still and it'll all happen to you anyway.' He winked. 'Don't want to rush things, after all.'

'Whatever,' Peter said dismissively. 'You don't have to rush things. You've got for ever to make bad choices, haven't you?'

The man guffawed, his mouth opening wide and his face getting even redder than before. Then he leant in close so that his rasping voice resonated in Peter's ear, making it itch. 'You talk about choices,' he said, his tone conspiratorial. 'But there's only one choice I want to make, and I can't make it, see? I don't want to die. I just can't see the point in living either.' He rolled his eyes and laughed, then slammed his empty glass down on the bar. 'Another of your finest,' he said to the barman, who duly filled the glass.

Peter looked at him for a moment, then he pushed back his stool. 'Maybe you can't,' he said angrily, 'but I can. And I'm going to.'

He stood up straight, his hands catching the bar to maintain his balance. As he did so, his eyes were drawn briefly to the ring on his finger with its engraved flower. The flower had always represented something important to him – not just his beginnings, but life itself. The Coveys had told him again and again about the natural cycle of life – flowers growing, blooming, spreading their pollen via butter-flies, bees and other insects in order to create their young before they died, their work done. They'd given him books on natural history, on natural selec-tion, on the development of a species through the cycle of life, reproduction and death. But Peter could see the ring was out of date now. The cycle had been broken; it wasn't relevant any more. Natural selection had been replaced by something else, something different, and there was no going back. It was still about survival of the fittest, though, and Peter was determined to survive, whatever it took. Without looking back at the man, Peter stumbled out of the bar. He needed to talk to Anna. He needed to know she'd survive with him.

'Peter!' Anna greeted him like a war hero, in spite of the fact that it was nearly midnight; in spite of the fact that he stank of alcohol, that he was swaying from side to side. It made him feel guilty, uncomfortable; he'd have preferred her to be angry with him.

'Hi,' he said, stumbling slightly. 'Sorry I'm late.'

Anna smiled cautiously. 'It's fine,' she said, 'I knew you'd be OK. Where were you?'

Peter shrugged. He'd been telling himself all the way home that he would sit Anna down the moment he got to the house; would tell her what he'd discovered. But now, looking at her worried face, her wide, trusting eyes, somehow he couldn't do it, couldn't find the words to tell her what he'd discovered. So instead, he pushed past and made his way to the kitchen.

'Ben's asleep, and I made shepherd's pie,' Anna said, eyeing him cautiously. 'It'll be cold now but I can reheat it. So, you've been drinking?'

'Shepherd's pie,' Peter said, sitting down heavily and noticing that the room was spinning. 'Great.'

'Were you with the Underground?'

Peter looked up briefly to see that Anna was looking at him hopefully; as he met her eyes, her voice trailed off. Then he remembered something and started to rummage through the pile of papers on the side of the table. Eventually he found what he was looking for.

'Our Declarations,' he said seriously, his voice slurring slightly. Anna nodded, and didn't say anything.

Peter blinked several times to try to force his eyes to focus. He began to read his again, managing the first few lines, then giving up when he realised he was seeing double.

Anna tentatively put a plate full of steaming hot shepherd's pie in front of him.

'You know everyone signs the Declaration, don't you?' Peter said, picking up his fork, then putting it down again. 'You know all that stuff Pip told us is bullshit?'

'No, it isn't,' Anna said lightly.

Peter raised an eyebrow. He didn't mean to go on the offensive, but he couldn't seem to stop himself. 'Even your parents signed it.'

Anna blanched. 'They didn't know what they were doing. They were young. They wished they hadn't.'

'They still signed.'

'What's the matter, Peter? Why are you talking like this? It's like you're . . .'

'Like I'm a Pincent? Well, I am. I'm Richard Pincent's grandson. Albert Fern's great-grandson. My family invented Longevity, Anna. Maybe it's in my blood.'

Anna's eyes widened in shock. 'It's not in your blood. You hate the Pincents. We're going to Opt Out, Peter. You know we are.'

He was being cruel. He hated himself for it. He took a mouthful of shepherd's pie. 'And achieve what? Die young, before we can make a difference? Why should we? Why shouldn't we stay around like everyone else?'

'Because we have to make room for new people,' Anna gasped. 'We're going to create a New Generation. You know that. What's wrong with you?'

'What's so great about new people?' Peter interrupted. 'And what if we can't . . . I mean, what if there is no new generation? What then?'

'I don't know what you mean,' Anna said, her face setting into the expression Peter remembered from Grange Hall – part stubborn, part afraid.

'Of course you don't. How could you?' Peter replied, his anger turning into bitterness, and self-loathing because he knew he was taking his anger out on the one person who was entirely blameless. 'You know nothing. You're too naive, that's your problem. You believe whatever you've been told. What your parents told you. What Mrs Pincent told you. What I told you. But it's all rubbish, Anna. I can't believe you can't see that.'

Anna swallowed and he could see the pinprick of tears in her eyes.

'It's not rubbish,' she said, her voice cracking just slightly. 'And I'm not naive. You've been drinking and you don't know what you're saying and I wish you'd shut up.'

'Maybe I should,' Peter said, standing up, refusing to meet her eyes. 'That's what Pip wants me to do, I'm sure. Just shut up and do what I'm told and not ask any difficult questions.'

'Pip? But he's on our side. He's helping us . . .'

'Right,' Peter said sarcastically. 'Do you think he'll help us if we sign the Declaration? Do you think he'll be on our side then?'

'No!' Anna was standing up now, fire in her eyes that Peter hadn't seen for a long time. 'No, he won't. Because it won't happen. Don't talk like this, Peter. You're scaring me. We won't sign. We'll never sign. We're going to have children, and they won't be Surpluses. They'll never be Surpluses.'

Peter stared at her, trying to put into words all the thoughts and feelings that crowded his head. He knew the truth. There would be no children. There would only ever be the two of them and Ben. There was no reason not to sign any more, no reason to die. But he couldn't tell her. Not yet.

'If you loved me, you'd sign.' He flung the words at her, kicking his chair and storming out of the kitchen.

'Peter . . .' Anna called after him, but he barely heard her as he stomped off to the sitting room, collapsed on the sofa and fell into a deep, dreamless sleep.

*

'Peter?'

Peter looked up, disoriented. He squinted at the face in front of him, at the familiar eyes staring down at him.

'Pip?'

'Anna called me. She said you'd been drinking. She sounded very worried about you.'

'She called you?' Peter pulled himself up and looked at Pip incredulously. 'And you came here? What about code names? What about security?'

'An emergency is an emergency. And don't worry, I was careful,' Pip said. Music was playing; Peter looked around and saw that the radio was on. Of course it was, he thought to himself bitterly. Pip never missed a trick. 'Anna said you were confused,' Pip continued. 'I'd like to help.'

'Well she's wrong,' Peter said angrily, moving his head and realising that he was still intoxicated. 'I'm not confused about anything. I told her we were going to sign the Declaration. Anyway, what are you doing here out in the open? I thought you only hung around darkened rooms, feeling important.'

'You want to sign the Declaration?' Pip's voice was steady, flat, and it drove Peter into a rage.

'You want to give me one reason why I shouldn't?' he asked bitterly, standing up suddenly, then gripping the side of the sofa to keep his balance. 'You want to tell me that the Surplus Sterilisation Programme never happened? You want to tell Anna that after all the crap you've been feeding us about "being the revolution" and "parenting the future children of the world" she's never going to have a child? That she can't because her insides have been ripped out or put to sleep or turned off, or whatever it is they've done to her? Because I can't.'

Pip was looking at him strangely. 'The programme. It's really true? It happened? How do you know? How did you find out?'

Peter didn't say anything for a few seconds. Even through his anger he'd harboured some small hope that there might be an explanation, that Pip might not have known. 'I saw the report,' he said eventually, his voice low and bitter. 'Saw our names on the list.' He looked at Pip in disgust. 'You knew,' he said, shaking his head. 'I thought you must know; you say you know everything. But then I thought no, you couldn't know, because if you even suspected something, you'd have told us. You wouldn't have allowed us to Opt Out of the Declaration, to build our whole lives around having children, when you knew full well we couldn't have any. I thought you weren't that much of a bastard. But I'm guessing I was wrong. Maybe you're the one who's outlived his usefulness, Pip. Ever thought about that?'

He could see Pip's eyes widen slightly, even in the darkness of the sitting room, lit only by a glimmer of moonlight through the window. Guilt, Peter thought to himself. Or perhaps just the shock of being found out.

'Peter, you must listen. There was talk of such a

programme but we understood that it had been abandoned. But even if this tragedy came to pass, there's still reason to Opt Out. To make a statement. You, of all people. Eternal life was never the destiny of mankind, Peter. We must fight the dogma that death is wrong, that nature's cycle can be ignored.'

'Like you, you mean?' Peter asked, his eyes flashing. 'Oh, no. That's right. You signed the Declaration, didn't you? Living for ever isn't something you were prepared to sacrifice, is it? Just me. Just Peter Pincent.'

Pip frowned uneasily. 'Peter, you know very well that I have no interest in prolonging my own life, in watching all this misery unfold; but my role in the resistance meant I had to sign the Declaration to ensure that the movement could develop. I couldn't risk it dying out. I live for the cause, that is all.'

'You mean you couldn't risk leaving it to the next generation to run the Underground in case they rejected your ideas,' Peter spat. 'You're as bad as the Authorities. All you care about is your own self-interest. Well, screw you. I've had enough. You never do anything anyway. As far as I can see, Pincent Pharma isn't exactly afraid of you.'

Pip's brow furrowed. 'I'm sorry you feel this way. I have never sought to be important, only to protect mankind from the terrible temptation of eternal life, only to fight for the new, for the young. I was going to contact you tomorrow anyway, Peter, because I have information about Pincent Pharma that I wanted you to investigate. A Unit X on the sixth floor. We are very concerned about what's happening there.'

'Unit X?' Peter put his hands in his pockets. 'You tell me nothing for weeks and now that I've finally seen through you, you tell me about a Unit X? I'm not an idiot, Pip. I've had enough. I think you should go.'

He opened the sitting room door to leave; Pip stood up.

'Peter, don't walk away from me. You're making a mistake. For Anna as much as yourself.'

Peter turned back, his eyes flashing. 'Don't you talk to me about Anna,' he said, his voice low and hoarse. 'Not after this. And don't you even think about contacting her again. We're going to sign, and we're going to be happy. You make one move and I'm telling the Authorities everything about you. I want you to leave us alone, Pip, do you understand? Just leave us alone.'

'I understand.' Pip's voice was gentle; sad rather than angry. 'But I am here for you, Peter. I will always be here.'

'Whatever,' Peter said, pushing past him and making his way up the stairs towards the bedroom. 'You can see yourself out.'

Then, remembering something, he turned back. 'I got your message, by the way. File 23b, wasn't it?' Casually, he pulled it out from under his waistband and threw it down the stairs.

'Message?' Pip had followed Peter from the sitting

room into the hallway. 'What message?'

'Consider it my last job for the Underground. Consider us quits.'

'Wait, Peter. I don't know what you mean. I didn't ask you for a file . . .' Pip called after him, but Peter had already reached the top of the stairs and turned the corner. And as he crept slowly towards the bedroom, his anger turned to desperation. The tears that had tried so hard to fall earlier began to stream from his eyes, as he did his best to fight them back.

'I'm sorry,' he begged, as he got into bed and pulled Anna towards him. 'I don't deserve you. I'm sorry.'

'Of course you deserve me,' Anna whispered, turning and wrapping her arms around him. 'Everything's going to be OK.' And Peter squeezed her back tightly, tighter than ever before, because he knew it wouldn't, because he knew that things would never be OK again.

Chapter Fourteen

Anna carefully manoeuvred Ben's battered pram down the steps leading to the high street, and followed the road round until she reached Angler's Way, where the Bright Days coffee shop was situated, and where she was due to meet Maria. It didn't feel like a bright day. It felt like a horrible, black, gloomy day, even if the sun was doing its best to shine through the clouds. Peter had left early that morning, had said nothing about the night before, had given her no reassurance that everything would be OK, that things would return to normal. Pip had assured her that he would be watching closely, that she shouldn't worry. But she did worry; she worried all the time. She felt like a balloon, felt as if Peter was losing his grip on her, that any minute now she'd be floating away into oblivion, alone and helpless in a never-ending sky.

As she entered the coffee shop, she saw Maria sitting at a small table in the window and she waved, relieved to see a friendly face, a face that didn't seem disappointed in her or angry for no reason. Maria immediately stood up and helped her navigate Ben through the closely clustered tables, then smiled benevolently at him. 'Such a handsome young man,' she said sadly. 'Such a shame he won't have any friends to play with.'

The smile on Maria's face was so sweet, so warm, and Anna felt her eyes well up. She longed to talk to someone about Peter, to hear a comforting voice telling her that his anger, his words, had meant nothing, but instead she wiped the tears away briskly and sat down, ordering a cup of sweet tea for herself and a glass of milk for Ben.

'You know, I am so very grateful you came,' Maria said, once the waiter had moved away. 'You've been through such a lot already. There's no reason why you should have to worry about other Surpluses.'

Anna shook her head. 'Of course I have to,' she said firmly, her confidence slowly returning. 'Peter and I were lucky. But there are lots of Surpluses who aren't so lucky. Who are still in Halls, who . . .' She winced as she spoke; she could almost smell the stale, institutional air of Grange Hall.

'Who need our help,' Maria whispered, then moved closer to Anna. 'What I want to ask you, Anna . . . you can say no. I want to make that very clear. I don't expect anything from you – you've been through so much and I know you've got a great deal on your plate, with Ben and everything.'

Anna nodded seriously, and felt the hairs on the back of her neck stick up slightly as they always did when she knew something important was going to happen.

'The thing is, Anna, there are children being hidden all across the country – by their parents, by relatives, by sympathisers. But it's getting more and more difficult.'

'You're . . . you're hiding children? Surpluses, you mean?'

Maria nodded. 'We prefer to describe them as children and young people,' she said cautiously.

'Like my parents,' Anna said breathlessly. 'Are you . . . do you work for the Underground?'

Maria frowned. 'No, Anna. We . . . we prefer to keep ourselves separate from the Underground.'

'But the Underground could help you! They helped me and Peter. They helped my parents. Really, I could make contact for you . . . if you want?'

Maria shook her head. 'Anna, when you're involved in something as dangerous as this, it's important to keep the number of people involved very small. It's just a matter of trust.'

'You don't trust the Underground? But that's silly. They're the only people you *can* trust.'

Maria's mouth twisted slightly. 'Perhaps. And I know they helped you and your parents. But other Surpluses in their protection have been found. I'm sure they have their priorities, but we're not interested in revolution. We just want to protect the children.'

Anna felt her chest constrict. 'You think the Underground don't?'

Maria bit her lip. 'I just think that sometimes it's safer to act alone.'

Anna took a few seconds to digest this information.

'And what is it you're doing? What can I do to help?'

Maria looked around furtively; the coffee shop was full, but no one appeared to be paying them any attention.

'We want to break into the Surplus Halls,' she said, when she seemed satisfied that no one was listening. 'We want to help the children in them escape.'

Anna's eyes widened and her heart was pounding in her chest. 'You want to break into Grange Hall? It's impossible. There're guards, Catchers . . .'

'I know that, Anna. I do. But we thought . . . if you could get out, then we can get in. Create a diversion. Then, when everyone's looking the other way, we'll get the Surpluses out.'

'Get them out?' Anna's head filled suddenly with images of Grange Hall, with the cold, bleak corridors, the small dormitories, the low ceilings, and she shuddered. 'But . . . but . . .'

'We need plans, layouts; we need to know how you got out, Anna,' Maria was saying.

Anna shook herself. 'You'll never manage it,' she whispered. 'They'll catch you. They'll send you to prison.'

'Perhaps. But that's a chance we have to take. Someone's got to do something, Anna. Even if we fail, people will hear about what we did. The Authorities will realise they can't ignore us.'

Anna took a deep breath. Maria was right. It was always worth trying. Peter had taught her that – if she hadn't believed him, she'd still be behind the walls of Grange Hall herself. 'Peter had a map,' she said tentatively. 'From the Underground. We got out through Solitary. In the basement. But they'll have closed it now. The tunnel, I mean.'

'Of course, but that's still of great use. Do you know how they got the map? Does Peter still have it?'

'I don't know about how they got it. Someone at the Authorities, maybe. I think Peter's still got it, though. I'm sure he has.' Anna looked up at Maria anxiously. 'But where will you take the Surpluses? How will you keep them safe?'

'The children, you mean,' Maria corrected her, leaning over Ben's pram and stroking his head. 'People will look after them. People like us.' She stood up to go. 'Thank you, Anna. I knew that you were good and courageous. As soon as I saw your face, I knew you were someone I could trust. I'll be in touch, and until then, you look after this little man, won't you?'

She pressed Anna's hand, then turned and left, leaving Anna staring after her. It was madness, she thought to herself. You couldn't just break into Grange Hall. You couldn't get five hundred Surpluses out secretly and keep them hidden.

But then again, she'd told Peter it was futile trying to escape, and they'd done it, hadn't they? Slowly, she picked up her tea and took a sip, wondering how to mention the map to Peter, bearing in mind his present mood. She decided that perhaps she wouldn't say anything for the time being; for now she'd keep Maria's plan to herself.

Chapter Fifteen

After what had felt like the longest morning he'd ever experienced, Peter stared listlessly at his chicken stew with extra iron and the tranqua-smoothie which his palm print had ordered for him; it was supposed to both boost his immune system and lower his blood pressure. What he really needed, though, was something to relieve the pain in his head and the feeling of nausea that crept through his body every time he thought of Anna, of the Declaration, of the choice that lay before him.

'I didn't know you were stressed,' Dr Edwards said, sitting down and eyeing the smoothie. 'Anything you'd like to talk about?'

Peter shook his head. 'I'm fine,' he said flatly. 'Those machines don't know what they're talking about.'

Dr Edwards smiled. 'I see. Hundreds of years of research and technological development dismissed out of hand. Well, I suppose you could be right. But then again, your dilated pupils, the frown lines above your eyes and the fact that you've been staring at your food for a full five minutes without even picking up a spoon suggest to me that perhaps the machine might know what it's talking about. So to speak.'

His eyes were twinkling, but Peter was in no mood for his humour.

'Fine,' he said stiffly. 'I'll have my tranqua-smoothie.' He picked it up and drank some – to his surprise, it was delicious. He intended to put it down after one or two gulps, but somehow the instruction didn't reach his hand or his mouth and moments later, the glass was drained. He put it down and sat back in his chair; he felt warm, nourished, slightly light-headed, a bit like he'd felt years ago when he first met the Coveys, when they put him to bed and read him a story and told him that he'd be safe with them.

He started to eat his stew.

'I take it your mood is not related to the codes I had you memorising this morning?' Dr Edwards asked, then he sat back in his chair. 'I'm sorry. It's really none of my business. If you don't want to talk, you don't have to.'

'I don't,' Peter said firmly, putting his spoon down. Then he studied Dr Edwards' face cautiously. Actually, he did want to talk. The very fact surprised him.

'You know about the Surplus Sterilisation Programme?' he asked, a few moments later.

Dr Edwards frowned. 'Sterilisation? No, Peter. I can't say that I do. Is it new?'

'Not new.' Peter paused briefly, looking up at the cameras, then he lowered his voice. 'Just new to me.' He paused again, trying to swallow the lump that had appeared in his throat. 'Turns out I'm not going to be much use at propagating the human race after all. Nor is Anna. They sterilise Surpluses when they're caught. They just don't think to tell anyone.' He attempted a casual laugh; it came out sounding bitter and angry.

'Peter, I'm sorry. I had no idea.' Dr Edwards looked truly sympathetic; Peter just shrugged.

'Yeah, well,' he said, returning to his bowl and spooning more stew into his mouth. 'I guess I should have expected something like that.'

'How could you expect that? It must be very difficult for you.'

Peter thought for a moment.

'Kind of.' He put his spoon down and looked up at Dr Edwards, at his kind smile and worried eyes. 'It's worse for Anna,' he said quietly. 'She's set on the idea of having children, thinks that it's her purpose in life or something.'

'And you?'

'Me?' Peter cleared his throat, playing for time. 'I don't know what my purpose is,' he said eventually. 'Maybe I don't even have one.'

'Of course you have one. And Anna will find a new one, I'm sure of it.'

'Anna doesn't know yet.'

'Ah. Now I understand the machine's reading.'

'I want her to understand.'

'To understand?'

Peter bit his lip. 'That it isn't my fault. That I didn't want this . . .'

'You feel guilty?'

'No. Maybe. I don't know how to tell her. I don't know where to start.'

'I think you won't know until you've tried. Why don't you go now?'

'Really?' Peter looked up hopefully.

'Really. You're a good student, Peter, but you're not invaluable. Not yet, anyway.'

To his surprise, Peter found himself grinning. He felt so much better. Unburdened. Light. And warm, in a fuzzy kind of way. 'Thanks, Dr Edwards. Thanks very much. I'll . . . I'll see you tomorrow.' Standing up, Peter made his way out of the canteen, swaying slightly as he walked. As he brushed by tables, knocking into one or two, he realised that he no longer viewed the other people eating lunch as enemies. One or two of them even smiled at him as he walked past. If he signed the Declaration and took Longevity, he found himself thinking, would he still be here in a hundred years, or would he be somewhere else completely? The questions floated around his head, but they didn't vex him. He felt calm, confident and self-assured for the first time in a very long time. He felt sure that he could win Anna over. After all, he thought to himself as he left Pincent Pharma and waved briefly at the smiling security guard, he had all the time in the world to do it.

Peter was humming as he approached the house. His despair from the night before felt alien and strange now, like a bad dream. He felt sure that Anna would see things as he did, that she, too, would embrace the chance to live for ever, once she'd got over her initial disappointment. Even their house didn't look quite so bad that morning – sure, it was still a complete hole, but it was their hole. It was their home, for now, until they were ready to move on. And they would be moving on soon, he was sure of it. He was going to achieve something with his life; he was going to make some money and within a few years he'd be able to move them out of the suburbs, whatever the Authorities had to say about it. He'd buy a bigger house where Ben had room to play and he'd fill it with books for Anna. Perhaps they'd travel, too – Anna had always said that she wanted to see the desert and now that they had for ever stretching out ahead of them, they could go there for as long as she pleased. They'd take a boat or a train; it would be an adventure. One of many adventures. They'd never get bored because they'd never stop discovering new things, never stop exploring and learning. Longevity wasn't bad in itself; it was just that most people were ignorant and dull and they didn't know how to use their time. They sat around worrying about their wrinkles instead of seeing their long lives as a huge opportunity. He and Anna would be different. He and

Anna would make every minute count. He and Anna would make something of themselves.

Pulling out his keys, Peter opened the door and sauntered into the kitchen. Anna, who was on the floor playing with Ben, looked up in shock.

'Have you been fired?' she asked, her eyes wide. 'What happened? How dare they?'

Peter grinned. 'Don't worry. I haven't been fired; I was just given a few hours off for good behaviour.'

'Good behaviour?' Anna looked perplexed.

'Hello, little one!' Peter scooped Ben into his arms and held him above his head, smiling as Ben squealed in delight. Then, handing Ben back to Anna, he pulled a box out of his bag. 'Chocolates,' he said. 'Thought you might like them.'

'Thank you!' Anna took his gift, her eyes still following him uncertainly. 'And you're sure everything's all right?'

'Of course.' Peter pulled out a chair from the table and sat on it. Then he looked at Anna, seriously. 'Listen, I'm sorry about yesterday. I was an idiot.'

Anna's face flushed. 'No, you weren't. You were just tired. It must be awful working at Pincent Pharma, Peter. But you can't let it get to you. We don't have to sign the Declaration. There are still people fighting. There are still people who care about Surpluses and nature. Really there are.'

'It's not that,' Peter said, smiling awkwardly. 'I mean, I know there are people fighting. And that's great. But it doesn't mean everyone has to . . . It doesn't mean that Opting Out is the only way.'

Anna's brow wrinkled in incomprehension and she pulled Ben to her. 'But I don't see how it isn't,' she said. 'Signing the Declaration means agreeing not to . . . It means you extend your own life in place of new life. It's against Mother Nature. It's . . . it's wrong, Peter. It's because of the Declaration that there are Surpluses. It's because of the Declaration that there are Catchers and mothers crying themselves to sleep because their babies were taken from them. It's because of the Declaration that Grange Hall exists . . .'

Her voice had grown smaller and her face was hot. Peter took a deep breath.

'The thing is, Anna, sometimes people don't have a choice. And that changes things.'

Why was he so weak, he chastised himself. Why couldn't he just tell her?

'Everyone has a choice,' Anna said. Her voice was still quiet, but there was steel in it.

'Not everyone.' He cleared his throat, which had suddenly grown tight. Ben started crying, and Anna stood up, jigging him about and soothing him.

'Is that what they told you at Pincent Pharma?' she asked darkly, not meeting his eyes. 'Is that what your grandfather said? You can't trust him, Peter, you know that. You can't trust anyone. Not even the Underground. Not necessarily.'

Peter stared at her strangely then remembered his argument with Pip the night before. He wondered how much she had heard of it.

'Do you trust me?' he asked. The tranqua-smoothie's effects were beginning wear off; Peter could feel his muscles tightening, could hear his voice becoming slightly strangled, insecure.

Anna nodded. 'Of course I do. I trust you completely.'

'You'd sign the Declaration if I asked you to?'

'You'd never ask me,' Anna said, looking intently at Ben. 'You hate Longevity. You hate Pincent Pharma. You hate . . .'

Peter looked at her, at her pale translucent skin, at the fiery determination in her eyes – the same determination he'd fallen in love with the first time he'd seen her. Even within the confines of Grange Hall, she'd managed to retain an air of dignity, of authority; now, he couldn't bear to be the one to strip it away, and he dropped his head into his hands.

'What I hate is that you don't know the truth. Anna, we don't have a choice,' he said. 'The Underground lied to us.'

'I don't know what you mean,' Anna said, shaking her head firmly. 'We have to Opt Out. We are the Next Generation and we'll be the parents of the generation after us. We're going to live for ever through our children. That's how it's meant to be, Peter. It's what you said. You know that.'

'Anna, we can't have children.' He said it almost silently, and afterwards he couldn't be entirely sure that he'd spoken the words at all. Anna was looking at him helplessly, confused. 'We can't have children because of the Surplus Sterilisation Programme,' he continued, finding the courage from somewhere to look her in the eye as he spoke. 'I found out about it yesterday. I . . .'

Slowly, Anna's face changed from incomprehension to disbelief. Peter pulled out the report, the report he'd stolen from his grandfather, and handed it to her. She put it on the table in front of her, staring at it blankly.

'There's nothing we can do,' Peter continued. 'The Authorities did it. At Grange Hall.'

'No.' Anna's voice was unrecognisable. 'No, it's not true.'

'It's OK, Anna,' Peter found himself saying. 'Because we'll still be together. And we'll have for ever to make a difference.'

'I don't want for ever,' Anna whispered. She was shaking; her eyes were slightly glassy.

'You just need to get used to the idea, Anna,' Peter said quickly, grabbing her hands to try to calm her. He had to make her see, had to open her eyes to the possibilities so she could see things as he did. 'Longevity's amazing – it's incredible, actually. And we'll have time to do everything you've ever wanted to do. We can go to the desert. We can travel around the world. You can read every book that's ever been written, and write a million, too.'

'I don't understand,' Anna said, her voice barely audible. 'Why are you saying this?'

'Anna, you have to know the truth. I was angry

too, but it happened. Even Pip knew about it. He wanted us to Opt Out, Anna, even though we can't have children, just to stick two fingers up at the Authorities. It's the Underground who lied.'

Anna's eyes returned to the piece of paper in front of her, then flickered around the room. And then her mouth opened and she let out a moan so loud, so guttural, Peter could hardly believe it was emanating from her.

'No,' she screamed. 'No. Please, no. Please . . .'

Her face was contorted, flushed, and Peter flinched.

'I'm sorry,' he whispered. 'I'm as sorry as you are, believe me.'

But instead of nodding, as he'd hoped, instead of accepting their fate as he had done, Anna pushed back her chair and stood up, her face scornful and her eyes as black as thunder. 'You're not sorry,' she shouted, desperately. 'You're pleased. You've changed, Peter. You've become like them. You want me to sign the Declaration and I won't. I'll never sign, Peter, not as long as I live. I won't . . .' She stared at him for a few seconds, as if to come up with the right words, her body shaking as she stood in front of him.

'I haven't changed,' Peter implored, trying to convince himself as well as her, wondering who was listening to this conversation, what they were thinking. 'I've just seen the light. Be sensible, Anna. You have to. I need you. It's you and me, together. I can't do it without you, Anna. Please don't leave me.'

'You're the one who's leaving,' Anna said, shaking

174

her head at Peter, reinforcing all his self-doubt, all his self-loathing. 'I won't ever sign, Peter. I don't care what you say.'

As Peter looked at her, he could feel a black, silent rage rising up inside him, because she wouldn't understand, because of what he was doing to her.

'You know,' he said, his voice bitter, 'I've never trusted anyone. Not until I met you. And I thought I could depend on you, I really did. But now . . . I should have known you'd let me down in the end too. Thanks, Anna. Thanks for nothing.'

He looked away from her, couldn't bear to see the hurt in her eyes. She stood in front of him for seconds, minutes – he wasn't sure. And then, silently, clutching Ben to her, she left the kitchen and ran up the stairs, slamming the bedroom door behind her.

Chapter Sixteen

The next day Peter woke feeling unrested, listless. Anna was already up; he could hear her pottering around the kitchen, could hear her chatting to Ben. She sounded so at ease, so comfortable, and yet he knew that the minute he went downstairs the veneer would crack, to be replaced by tension, by anger, by denial. All he'd done was tell her the truth and now he felt betrayed, pushed out, deserted.

Eventually, he forced himself out of bed, delaying the moment where he'd have to face her by taking a shower, scrubbing himself all over, then getting dressed silently. He had his coat on by the time he walked into the kitchen; the sooner he was out the door, the better.

Anna looked up and he could see that she had been crying.

'You don't want breakfast?' she asked, avoiding his eyes, her voice tinged with reproach.

He shook his head. 'I'm running late. Better get to work.'

Anna nodded and turned back to Ben.

'So I'll see you later, then,' Peter said, forcing his eyes away from her.

'OK.'

She didn't turn around; Peter shrugged and walked towards the front door, banging it loudly behind him. By the time he arrived at Pincent Pharma, his mood had worsened; it was not improved by the fact that his grandfather was waiting for him in the lab.

'Dr Edwards tells me you're signing the Declaration.'

Peter started slightly, then frowned and looked over at Dr Edwards, whose expression was unreadable.

'He did?' Peter took off his coat and hung it up on a hook, careful not to react, forcing himself not to say anything he'd regret.

'You've made the right decision.'

'Turns out I didn't have much of a choice.'

His grandfather stared at him levelly for a few seconds. 'Peter,' he said, 'I understand that you came by some information. Something that I was hoping I wouldn't have to tell you until after you'd signed for the right reasons. I am unclear as to how you came by it. Nevertheless, I think in the circumstances that these issues might be overlooked.'

'Right. Thanks.'

Peter shot a furtive look at Dr Edwards who was staring at him curiously.

'So you're definitely signing?' His grandfather was looking at him intently; Peter swallowed uncomfortably. 'Because I was thinking that we should celebrate it. Hold a press conference, perhaps . . .'

'I'm not signing.' Peter's voice was flat.

'Not signing?'

'No.'

There was a pause. 'I see.' His grandfather's face was impassive. 'Well, isn't that a shame. Any particular reason?'

Peter didn't say anything; his grandfather, though, didn't appear to need to hear the reason out loud. 'It's the girl, isn't it? She's stopping you.'

Peter's continued silence was all the answer he needed; Richard Pincent smiled tightly, and left the lab.

'I didn't realise the two of you were so close,' Peter said archly to Dr Edwards, and pulled on his lab coat.

Chapter Seventeen

It was mid-morning, and the house in Surbiton was silent; every so often the sound of a distant car could be heard, or the shrill voices of neighbours greeting each other on the street, but within the house itself nothing stirred. Ben was having his nap; the curtains were closed against the cold day, the sky dark and unwelcoming. Anna sat cross-legged on the sofa, her head in her hands, rocking back and forth in a movement that she could trace back to her time as a Small in Grange Hall, where the only comfort to be found had been the reassurance that you could provide yourself. She had been young – not even three – when she arrived at Grange Hall, and her memories of that time were very limited. Mostly she remembered feeling confused, desperate and alone as she gradually realised that the cold, dank top-floor dormitory was her new home; that no one was coming to get her.

Now, as she slowly rocked back and forth, she tried to reassure herself in the same way. For hours, all she had been able to conceive of was the gaping mouth of a vacuous, empty hell, a hell in which her womb was redundant, futile, in which she and Peter would drift endlessly with nothing to ground them, no new life to nurture and watch over carefully. But Anna had learnt many years before that despondency and despair were the routes to nowhere good. Survival meant adaptation, acceptance, learning new rules as they were introduced, and Anna knew that the situation she now found herself in was no different. She would cope. She would find a way to make herself fit for purpose, for the new reality that had been imposed on her.

Next to her on the sofa, her Declaration lay spread out for her to sign – something that as yet she'd been unable to do. Every time she looked at it she felt a heavy revulsion force her eyes away, as though by signing it she would relinquish her soul, her very being; and yet, she kept telling herself, by signing she would transcend the fate of that little girl who had rocked to and fro on the top floor of Grange Hall, the little girl labelled 'Surplus' and told on a daily basis that Longevity was man's greatest invention, that she, as an illicit entrant into this world, had no right to benefit from it. Several times, she'd picked up her pen to sign; several times she'd forced herself to bring the pen down on the Declaration, to think of Peter, to try and write her name, but each time she'd dropped it, tears cascading down her cheeks. She couldn't do it. Something deep inside of her was forcing the pen from her hands; some power within was determined to stop her. Peter was right – she was letting him down, and it made her feel sick to her core.

So she sat and she rocked, allowing her mind to empty, allowing herself to be seduced by the gentle rhythm until everything felt safer, until the world had all but disappeared.

It was only the doorbell that startled Anna from her trance, only its piercing ring that was able to shock her back into the real world. Ben was still sleeping – she checked her wrist and guessed that she had another twenty minutes before he awoke, demanding to be plied with attention and love, demanding to be the centre of her world, something that she willingly allowed him. Ben's needs were so simple, she thought to herself as she wrapped a cardigan around herself and walked towards the front door. They were so easy to fulfil, so reassuring in their urgency. Peter's needs, on the other hand, were much more complex and fraught with danger, like a field of landmines that she wanted desperately to grow flowers on; one false move and it would blow up in her face.

The glass panels on the front door to their house were opaque; it wasn't until she'd opened it that she realised who it was. Her first reaction was to go white.

'Peter . . . is he OK? Is something wrong?'

Richard Pincent smiled benevolently. 'Peter is very well, Anna. Peter is extremely well, in fact. It was you I wanted to see. I wonder if I might come in?'

He stepped across the threshold before Anna could

decide whether or not to welcome him in, had given her his coat before she'd had time to offer to take it. A minute later, he was in the sitting room, sitting on their sofa; Anna hurriedly swept her Declaration off it, placed it face down on the floor.

'Would you . . . would you like some tea?' she asked. She had met Richard Pincent only once, the day her parents had died; he had come to take Peter away. To her eternal gratitude, Peter had chosen to stay with her, but Richard Pincent's face had for ever been etched into her memory, a figure to be feared.

'No, nothing, thank you. So this is your house?'

Anna nodded and sat down on the chair to the left of the sofa; she could think of no appropriate answer to such a question, was terrified that if she even opened her mouth she would say the wrong thing.

Richard Pincent smiled again. 'You know, Peter's turning out to be quite the scientist.'

Anna nodded apprehensively. He wasn't really here to talk about Peter, she was sure of it.

'Yes, he's a very intelligent young man,' Richard Pincent continued silkily. 'You must be very proud of him.'

Anna nodded again. Her feelings for Peter went beyond pride; they were of love in its purest sense, but not a love that could be described with terms like pride, respect, even adoration. Peter was part of her. Peter was the reason she breathed, the reason she got up each morning, the reason this strange, harsh world filled her with hope more often than complete and utter despair. At least, he had been.

'I'm very proud,' she said quietly.

Richard Pincent stood up, his expression sad and thoughtful. 'He really cares about you, Anna. He's told me, you know. I gather you had quite a time of it in Grange Hall.'

Anna watched silently, as he turned to look at a painting on the wall, a painting of sunflowers that Peter had picked up in a market for her, a painting that reminded her of her parents' house – sunny and warm and light.

'And I wondered,' Richard continued, 'just how much you care about him.'

'How . . . how much I care about him?' Anna's voice caught slightly, with indignation, with outrage. How dare he ask her how much she cared for Peter? How dare he?

'Love, you see Anna, is a difficult thing. It means putting another person first. So often people talk of love, but what they mean is need and longing; they want to own the other person, subjugate them to their will. Real love, well, it means sacrifice. It means thinking of the other person's needs before your own. Sometimes I wonder if real love still exists, but then I look at Peter, I hear him talk about you, and it chastens me. He does love you, Anna. Very deeply.'

'He does?' Anna knew that he did, but to hear the words still reassured her, even to hear them from Richard Pincent.

'Of course he does. So much, in fact, that he's

sacrificing himself for you. His life. His ambition.'

Anna's eyes widened. 'His life?'

Richard Pincent sat down again, this time at the other end of the sofa, closer to Anna. 'Peter has realised some things about himself, Anna, about the world. He's got so much to give, you see, so much to contribute. And Opting Out . . . it would constrict him, it would decimate his chances to do anything worthwhile. Your parents, Anna, had a huge influence over my grandson. I'm eternally grateful to them for keeping him safe for me, and to you for being there for him. But I'm sure that you are grateful to him for helping you. I'm sure you can see that people change, people move on, that sometimes the loving thing to do is to set someone free, not to impose your own views on them, to restrict their choices.'

'I'd never restrict Peter,' Anna said, her voice hoarse and dry, uncertain. However much she hated Richard Pincent, he was right. Peter had trusted her, and she'd let him down. He'd saved her, and now she wasn't there for him. 'But I can't Opt Out. I can't.'

Richard Pincent nodded thoughtfully. 'I'm sure you believe that, Anna. I'm sure you think you're doing the right thing. But the problem is, your decision doesn't just affect you, does it?'

Anna wished he would go, wished he would leave her alone. 'It's still the right thing,' she managed to say. 'My parents . . . They died because of the Declaration . . .'

Richard Pincent nodded. 'Of course. Your parents.

It was very sad. Tragic, in fact. But they signed the Declaration themselves, didn't they?'

'Only because they didn't know what it really meant.'

'You believe that?' Richard frowned. 'They were your age, weren't they? Or older? I'm sure they must have understood it?'

'No,' Anna said fiercely. 'They thought they could Opt Out later. They wanted to have children . . .'

'Ah, children.' Richard nodded, thoughtfully. 'I understand. But if they couldn't have had children – then everything would have been OK, wouldn't it? There wouldn't have been anything wrong with them signing?'

'I don't know,' Anna said tightly. 'I know they didn't want me to sign, though. They joined the Underground to fight Longevity.'

Richard raised an eyebrow and Anna flushed at her realisation that she'd mentioned the Underground in front of Peter's grandfather. She clenched her fists to regain control over herself.

'Yes, the Underground,' Richard said levelly. 'Of course, you know that they are all criminals? And that association with such activity brings a prison sentence?'

Anna nodded. 'I know. Peter and I . . . we wouldn't . . . I mean . . .'

'I know you wouldn't do anything like that,' Richard said generously. 'And I'm sure your parents only turned to them out of love for you. They loved

Peter, too, didn't they?'

Anna nodded again.

'And he risked his life to come and save you from Grange Hall. Isn't that right?'

'Yes, he did,' Anna said, drawing her knees up on to her chair, pulling them into her chest.

'Yes, indeed,' Richard Pincent continued. 'Now, do you think it's possible that it's time for you to save Peter's life?'

'Save Peter's life?' Anna's eyes widened in fear. 'What's happened to him? What . . .'

'Oh, no, nothing. Don't worry,' Richard smiled. 'I meant that he listens to you. He cares about you. And as long as you won't sign the Declaration, he won't. But refusing to sign, you're cutting his life short. You're effectively killing him, Anna.'

'Killing him? No, I . . .' Anna said anxiously, then dug her nails further into the palms of her hands. 'Humans aren't meant to live for ever,' she managed to say eventually. 'They're just not.'

'I see,' Richard Pincent said, nodding slowly. 'Is that what you think? Really?'

Anna nodded uncertainly.

'I thought you loved Peter.'

'I do!' Anna said, her eyes widening. 'I do love him!'

'I doubt that,' Richard Pincent said sadly. 'If you loved him, you'd know that he's spent his entire life hiding, hampered, weighed down by his Surplus status. Now he's got the chance to reclaim his life, to really be a someone, but instead, he's being held back by you and your brother.'

'I'm not holding him back,' Anna said fretfully.

'Oh, but you are. And you will continue to do so if you don't sign the Declaration,' Richard said, his voice grave. 'By Opting Out, you jeopardise his health, your own health. I know what that means, Anna – my own wife died of cancer when she was just thirty. I spent a year watching her die, watching her waste away and it was the hardest thing I've ever had to do. It's what made me so determined to fight illness, to fight nature's relentless onslaught. Could you do that to Peter? Could you allow him to suffer if you were to get ill? Could you let him watch you die, knowing that it was your fault?'

Anna flinched. 'I wouldn't let him watch me die,' she said quietly. 'And I'm not stopping him from signing. He can if he wants.'

Richard Pincent shook his head. 'Peter is deeply committed to you and your brother,' he said softly. 'He's an honourable young man. A loyal one. He would never sign the Declaration, however much he wanted to, if you chose not to.'

Anna hung her head. 'But . . .' she whispered. 'But we have to be Opt Outs. We have to . . .' She felt her shoulders slump. Had to what? She asked herself miserably. They couldn't have children. They couldn't start the Next Generation. They were nothing.

'If you don't sign, you're sentencing Peter to an early death. To illness, possibly disability. Is that what you want?'

'No!' Anna shook her head vehemently. 'No, that's not what I want. I . . .'

'You want a family. I understand that, Anna. I'm very proud to have a grandson, particularly one as clever and courageous as Peter. But as I'm sure you know, it's impossible for the two of you to have children. It's desperately unfair, but this is the situation we find ourselves in. You have Ben though, don't you? I'm sure your parents wouldn't have wanted you to sacrifice Peter, or yourself, for nothing. Would they?'

Anna wrapped her arms around her stomach and had to force herself not to start rocking again. She thought of her parents, her kind, wonderful parents who had regretted signing the Declaration all their lives, because it had taken her away from them. She thought of Peter, imagined him staying with her out of loyalty, miserable because of her failings, because of the invisible chains linking them together. Then she looked at Richard Pincent. He had Mrs Pincent's eyes, the same way of staring at her, terrorising her, breaking her down until all she wanted was to please.

'I don't want Peter to sacrifice himself for me,' she managed to say. Tears were pricking at her eyes.

'Then you have to sign. Just sign the Declaration and Peter will have all the chances he deserves. Show him that you love him, Anna. Make the sacrifice that you know he'd make for you.'

Anna sniffed and wiped some stray tears away.

'I can help you, if you want,' Richard Pincent

continued. 'If you need someone to stand by you as you sign, to give you courage?'

Anna looked up at him hesitantly, feeling the resistance within her bones fighting with her love for Peter. She couldn't sign. Couldn't give up on everything her parents had fought for, and yet she knew she would, knew she had no real choice.

Slowly, tentatively, aware of every nerve in her body, feeling her legs shaking as they took her weight, Anna slipped off her chair and retrieved her Declaration from the floor. She stood, looking at it for a few moments, feeling a dead weight in her stomach as she scanned the words. Then, swallowing the bile that was rising up the back of her throat, she returned to her seat. Richard Pincent handed her a fountain pen.

'You're doing this out of love,' he said, watching beadily as Anna's trembling hand approached the document. 'Just think of the long and happy life you'll lead with Peter. So much time together. So much time . . .'

Her hand now shaking violently, Anna forced pen to paper, managed to scrawl something approaching her name. Then, dropping the pen and clutching her stomach, she ran from the room, making it to the bathroom just in time before she vomited again and again, her body erupting like an angry volcano. The noise soon woke Ben, whose desperate cries seemed to verbalise her feelings of despair, of having done something so terrible that no words could describe it.

Then, slowly, she pulled herself upright and splashed water on her face before she went into Ben's room and, leaning over him in his makeshift cot, she stroked him until his cries abated. Then she carefully made her way downstairs, to apologise to her guest. Her guest had gone, however. Quietly, discreetly, he'd left, closing the door behind him. And with him, Anna noticed immediately, had gone her Declaration.

Unsteadily, Anna walked towards the bookshelves and she took out a book she hadn't written in for a long time. Returning to the kitchen, she picked up her pen, a pen far cheaper than the one she'd used to sign her Declaration, and began to write.

My name is Anna. My name is Anna Covey and I have signed the Declaration. I'm not an Opt Out any more.

She stared at the words – they looked alien, wrong.

My name is Anna Covey and I'm going to live for ever. Peter and I are going to take Longevity and live for ever. And it's OK because we Didn't Have a Choice. It's OK, because I did it out of Love. Peter said

She sighed heavily, trying to remember why it was OK, trying to remember what Peter had said. She felt sick again, felt a sense of ominous dread rising up inside her and she picked up the phone to call Peter, for reassurance, but then she put it down again.

Instead, moments later, she dialled another number.

'Maria? It's Anna. I was just calling to say . . .'

She never finished the sentence, because her body started to shake violently, juddering sobs crashing up through her lungs, loud and raw.

Chapter Eighteen

Maria was waiting for Anna when she arrived; tea was already brewing and biscuits were laid out on the table. She hadn't sounded surprised to hear from her, had soothed her, helped her to focus, told her to come over immediately. Now, Maria pointed to the sofa, where Anna gratefully sat down, allowing the soft cushions to comfort her. Maria, meanwhile, took Ben and rocked him in her arms until he fell asleep. And then she looked up, her expression tentative, and said, 'So.'

'So,' Anna repeated, and sighed. 'So . . .'

She took a deep breath. 'Peter . . .' she started, but even as she said his name she could feel her stomach clenching at the thought of telling anyone anything about what she had done. Peter was hers, he was her hero, her everything; she would die for him if that's what it took, and here she was about to discuss him with a virtual stranger. It felt wrong, it felt like a betrayal.

'I can't have children,' she said instead, her eyes welling up with tears as she spoke. 'There was a

Surplus Sterilisation Programme. My name was on the list. Peter wanted to sign the Declaration. I had to. I love him. I don't want to restrict him. But . . . but . . .'

'You signed the Declaration?' Maria asked gently.

Anna nodded. 'I . . . I did it because I love him. But it feels wrong. Desperately wrong. Maybe I don't love him enough? Maybe he doesn't love me enough. Not now. Not any more.'

'I'm sure he loves you,' Maria said soothingly.

Anna looked up at her, and gave voice to the demons that had been circling her mind since she'd discovered the truth.

'But I'm useless,' she whispered. 'I can't have children.'

'That's not your fault. And he can't, either,' Maria said reasonably.

'We wanted to start the Next Generation,' Anna said, her voice becoming hoarse. 'That was the point. Of me, I mean, of us. My parents . . . they said that I was Nature's hope. That the human race could be reborn bit by bit. They died . . . They died so that I could live. To have children. They didn't know. If they'd known . . . they . . . they wouldn't have . . .'

'Oh, I think they would, Anna,' Maria said, moving closer. 'You were their child. They would want the best for you. Just as the rest of us want the best for our children. You can start the next generation by helping us, Anna. That's just as important as having children.'

Anna nodded seriously, and took out the map she'd

found amongst Peter's things. 'I brought the map, like you asked,' she said tentatively. 'I don't know if it will help, but . . .'

Maria took the map and studied it, her eyes lighting up. 'Anna, this will help enormously. Thank you. You see? You're not useless at all. Not one little bit.' She stood up and walked to the window, moving the curtain just slightly.

Anna forced a smile, but it didn't reach her eyes. 'Everything's so different now,' she whispered. 'I'm not sure I'm ready for it.'

'You will be,' Maria said, returning to her chair and handing Ben back to Anna. 'You'll find a way. You're strong, Anna. Strong people always find a way through their problems. They always find a way out.'

'You mean like Peter,' Anna said sadly. 'He was the one who found the way out of Grange Hall. Not me. I never thought you could get out. I never thought . . .'

She didn't finish her sentence. At that moment, the front door crashed open and three men burst through it. Maria immediately jumped up and ran from the room.

'Anna Covey?' another man asked. She nodded fearfully.

'You'd better come with us,' the man continued. 'And we'll take that,' he said, picking up the map that Maria had left on her chair.

Anna knew immediately that this was her fault; that she had done something terrible. 'I don't want to.'

The man laughed coldly as Ben was wrenched from her and she was handcuffed and dragged towards the door.

'Ben!' Anna screamed. 'Give him back. You can't do this. I'm Legal . . . I'm . . .'

'Legal? Don't make me laugh. You're Surplus, that's what you are,' the man said, throwing her towards the other man. 'A dirty little Surplus who thinks she can help the others to escape. Once a Surplus, always a Surplus. But don't worry. You're not going to prison. You're going somewhere much worse.'

'No. Please,' Anna begged, but her words were ignored, and all she could hear as she stumbled down the stairs was the sound of Ben's cries.

Chapter Nineteen

Pincent Pharma seemed bigger on the inside than it did on the outside. It was whiter, brighter, lighter than anywhere Jude had been in his life. Too light, Jude decided, squinting as he followed Derek Samuels past the escalator. He didn't like the place; preferred the darkness of his bedroom.

Derek Samuels was a thin-faced, wiry man with narrow shoulders and high eyebrows that turned everything he said into a question. He led Jude down a long white corridor, through some double doors and into another, narrower corridor. Eventually, he was shown into a small room with a table in it.

'Now,' Derek Samuels said, smiling thinly, 'would you like to tell me who you are and what you're doing here?'

Jude looked at him, an expression of boredom on his face. 'Like I said in my message, I'm offering to fix your security. I thought that's why you replied.'

Mr Samuels said nothing; he stood up.

'To fix our security,' he repeated, icily, then folded his arms and narrowed his eyes. 'As it happens, I have checked your references,' he said levelly. 'I know who you are, know who your father was, know what you've been doing for a living. What I want to know, though, is why you are here. And how you managed to hack into our systems. Who put you up to it? And what did they ask you to do?'

His voice was silky, but Jude could hear the threat behind it.

'No one put me up to it,' he said with a bored sigh. 'Hacking into systems is what I do. I managed to hack in because your systems need updating. Because they're old. Probably the people who developed them are old too. Where's Mr Pincent, anyway?'

'Old.' Mr Samuels moved closer. 'That's interesting.' He moved closer still, so that his face was only inches from Jude's. 'You know,' he said, his voice almost a whisper, 'what the best thing about Longevity is?'

Jude shook his head, felt his hands going clammy, tried to look anywhere but into Mr Samuels' eyes.

'It's that there aren't any young people cluttering up the world,' Mr Samuels continued. 'Thinking they know it all.' His face was expressionless, but Jude could hear the anger simmering in his voice, and suddenly found himself suppressing a little smile. Underneath that hard-man exterior, Mr Samuels was unsettled, he realised. Threatened by youth.

'Thinking?' Jude said levelly, his confidence returning. 'Well, in this case, I do know it all. All there is to know about security systems, anyway. Which you know, because otherwise you wouldn't have invited me in. So do you want me to get to work, or shall I go?'

Mr Samuels' eyes narrowed. 'How's your mother?' he asked, his eyes glinting slightly.

Jude stared back at him silently.

'Oh, that's right,' Mr Samuels continued. 'She left, didn't she? Went to . . . South America, was it? With her new husband? She left you all alone, didn't she? Probably couldn't wait to get away from you.'

Jude felt his heart quicken in surprise and anger; it took him a second to regain his composure. 'Leave my mother out of this.'

'And what about that Surplus brother of yours?' Mr Samuels smiled icily. 'Where does that leave you?'

Jude stared at him stonily. 'It doesn't leave me anywhere. It's no big deal.'

'No big deal?' Mr Samuels laughed, then his face contorted into a sneer. 'A few weeks, and you could have been the Surplus.'

Jude's face was angry, hot, red and it was all he could do to look straight ahead, to pretend that the very same thought hadn't dogged him for months. Ever since Peter's existence became national news. Ever since he escaped; ever since Jude's father was murdered by his former wife, Mrs Pincent, Peter's mother.

'Look, what's this about?' Jude said evenly, forcing himself to keep control. 'If you don't want me to look at your system, I think I'll be going now.'

'Oh, you're not going,' Derek Samuels said,

blocking his path. 'You're not going anywhere. The reason I got you in here today is that we're holding a rather important press conference. We've got a visit from the Authorities. And it is my job to ensure that nothing goes wrong. Absolutely nothing. To which end, I'm keeping you locked up until it's over, until I know you can't do any damage.'

'Locked up?' Jude looked at him incredulously. 'You can't lock me up.'

'Oh, but I can,' Samuels said. 'What you need to understand, Jude, is that I can do anything I like.'

The guard looked around him uncomfortably, before tentatively knocking on the blue door in front of him. He wasn't used to being in the ReTraining area of Pincent Pharma and felt out of place.

Cautiously, he listened for a response, but there was none. He knocked again, this time louder.

'Is that the door?' he heard a voice say. 'Hello? Is there someone there? Come in, please.'

Emboldened, he pushed the door open. Sure enough, as he'd been told, there were two people in the large white room: Dr Edwards, the one who worked all hours, never seemed to go home, and the boy. The Pincent boy.

'I've . . . well, I've got a delivery. For the boy,' he said, stumbling over his script.

'The boy?' Dr Edwards asked. 'You mean Peter?'

'That's right,' the guard said. 'For Peter. Peter Pincent.'

'Do you usually deliver mail?' Dr Edwards asked curiously. 'I thought you were security.'

'I am,' the guard said, reddening slightly, trying to remember exactly what he'd been told to say. 'Only this is valuable. It was hand delivered. By a young lady. Wanted to make sure it got to him safely. Peter Pincent, I mean. I just happened to be there.'

'Then shouldn't you perhaps be directing this at him?' Dr Edwards asked, his mouth curving up into a slight smile. The guard nodded curtly.

'Here,' he said, thrusting out the envelope in Peter's direction. Peter looked at it curiously.

'For me?' he asked.

The guard nodded. 'That's right.'

'And it's from who?'

'Young lady. The Surp— the one what you got out of Grange Hall with,' the guard said nervously. 'By the looks of her, at least. Same age as you, I'd have guessed.'

Peter looked shaken. 'When was she here? Can I still catch her?'

'I'm afraid I had some important business to attend to primarily.' The guard's eyes followed the envelope. 'She was here, what, forty minutes or so ago. Didn't want to stop, she said.'

'Is that all she said?'

The guard shook his head.

'What, then? What did she say?' Peter demanded.

'She said to tell you,' the guard said slowly, 'that you was right. That she was sorry. And that she'd see you later.'

'That I was right? She really said that?'

'And that she was sorry,' the guard confirmed. 'Now, if it's all right with you, I'd better be getting back to my post.'

'Of course,' Peter said, turning the envelope over in his hands. 'And thank you.'

'You're welcome,' the guard said, his hand caressing the hefty tip sitting in his trouser pocket. 'Just doing my job.'

Jude found himself in a small room, more like a cupboard. The walls were thick, the door solid and there were no windows; only an air vent in the ceiling provided the space with oxygen.

'You'll stay here,' Derek Samuels said. 'Not that you have a choice. You won't be going anywhere until I allow you to.'

'You think you're so clever,' Jude muttered under his breath.

'Borne out by experience,' Mr Samuels said smugly. He pulled out a walkie-talkie from his pocket. 'I need a guard. Room 25 on the ground floor.' Then he looked back at Jude. 'If I were you, I wouldn't do anything to upset him.' And then, shooting Jude one last, triumphant look, he opened the door with his identi-card and left, locking it behind him.

Angrily, Jude leant against the wall and allowed himself to slide down to the ground. Somewhere in the building, the red-haired girl was lying, like a princess in a twisted fairytale, unobtainable.

Somewhere else in the building, Peter Pincent was working. Jude, meanwhile, was stuck in a cupboard, trapped and impotent. Angrily he let out a sigh, then stood up again and kicked the wall with his foot. He'd thought he was so smart; had thought he knew it all.

And then he frowned. Maybe he did know it all. Well not all, perhaps, but enough. Derek Samuels hadn't searched him, after all. He still had his hand-held device. He cast his mind back to when he'd been sitting in his bedroom surveying Pincent Pharma through its security system. He'd had the blueprint of the building right in front of him. If he thought hard enough, he could probably remember how he'd got here from reception, then he could work out where he was. His brow furrowing, he found his eyes travelling up towards the air vent. It was small. Difficult to reach. And well sealed.

Jude scanned the room. And then his eyes lit up. In the corner, at the back of a shelf, a paint tin sat, discarded, and a painting tray with a scraping tool sitting in it, both caked in stark, white paint. One out of three problems solved. Listening out for the guard's footsteps, Jude picked up the scraper and, putting his foot on the shelf, he lifted himself up towards the ceiling.

Chapter Twenty

It took Jude a minute or so to get his bearings, and a couple more for his eyes to adjust to the dark. The only light came from the vents below him, which was barely enough to see by. The space above the ceiling was hot and dusty and full of cables, heating pipes and air-conditioning units; his progress was torturous and uncomfortable. But he scrambled as quickly as he could, stopping every few seconds to listen out for the beep of an identi-card opening the door to his cell. He had gone over his route from reception in his head and if he was correct, he was only a few metres from the Pincent Pharma Energy Centre, which was also on the ground floor, next door to the Security Centre.

Frantically, he crawled; he had only minutes, he knew that, and the seconds were ticking by. He didn't have long enough to find the girl, didn't have long enough to do anything, except . . . Except buy himself more time, Jude told himself.

Finally, he arrived at his destination. As he'd expected, above the Energy Centre the ceiling was crammed with devices, with wires, with routers and rerouters. Carefully, he looked around, then alighted upon the mainframe, the hosting computer that ran all of Pincent Pharma's energy supply. The monitors were below in the room itself where employees and guards sat; Jude could hear them talking. Little did they know that above them, the mainframe routes could be found, that by connecting them to his hand-held device, he had access to the only computer that really mattered. Feeling the sweat begin to drip from his forehead, he reached out towards it, took a deep breath and got to work.

The damage would have to be small, impossible to find but devastating in its impact he decided, as he bypassed security and navigated on to the system set-up. He could hear the sound of heavy footsteps in the corridor outside the Energy Centre, and had to wipe beads of sweat from his forehead. Something that would look like a power cut. Something that would shut everything down for at least twenty minutes ideally.

The seconds were ticking by – Jude knew that his absence might be discovered any minute. And then he found it. A connecting code, one of thousands of links embedded in the system. One change would render the system useless and it would take days, maybe even weeks, to find the error. Deftly, he changed one of the letters, keyed in a delay of ten minutes, then franti-cally, crawled back down towards his cell; twice he thought he had arrived back, only to find that the air vent beneath him was fixed in place. Finally, he found the vent that he'd taken out, swung back through it, and closed it behind him as best he could; as he landed on the ground, it fell open slightly. Quickly, he began to climb back up to fix it in place again, but stopped suddenly when he heard footsteps coming down the corridor. Dropping to the floor, he dusted himself down and looked up guiltily, just as the door swung open and a guard appeared, well-built, head shaven.

As he entered, he eyed Jude suspiciously.

'What's going on in here?'

'Nothing!' Jude did his best to hide his breathlessness, put all his effort into feigning the outrage and frustration that the guard would be expecting. 'What can go on? I'm in a cupboard. But if you don't let me out I'm going to scream blue murder.'

'Scream?' The guard grinned and pulled out a chair. 'You do that. No one'll hear you. These rooms have been soundproofed especially. You can scream all you like.'

'I want you to let me go,' Jude said angrily, trying to stop his eyes from darting involuntarily towards the air vent, which was dangling precariously. 'It's against the law to keep me here against my will. I've done nothing wrong.'

'Think the law applies at Pincent Pharma?' the guard asked. 'We make the law, is what we do.'

'I'll tell the Authorities.' Jude sat down, kicked his feet; he wanted the guard looking at him, nowhere else.

'And they'll pat us on the back for locking you up and keeping you out of mischief.' The guard yawned and sat down on his chair, then looked over at Jude, his blank eyes appearing to look straight through him. 'Now, shut up,' he said quietly, 'or I'll make you shut up. Got that?'

Jude nodded silently; he could hear the threat in the guard's voice, knew that he wouldn't need much of an excuse to drop the veneer of civility. He held his breath. Any minute now the air vent was going to fall, he knew it. His chest clenched as he waited for the minutes to tick silently by. One minute. Two minutes. Three minutes. And then, suddenly, the lights went out and they were plunged into darkness.

'What the . . .' the guard said, pulling out his walkie-talkie. 'Hello? 245 here. Request information on blackout in Room 25 . . . What? It's everywhere? . . . No, he's here with me. Must be something else. How the . . . Right, I'll check.' Jude heard him stand up, walk towards the door and pull it. 'It's open,' he said angrily. 'Bloody nightmare . . . I'll have to lock it using the override.' He sighed, then opened the door again and felt around the bottom. 'Be there in five minutes.'

'Everything all right?' Jude asked, doing his best to keep any note of triumph out of his voice.

'Everything's fine,' the guard snapped. 'Just an electrical fault. Lucky for you this door locks the old-fashioned way too. So whilst I'm required elsewhere, you'll be nice and safe in here on your own. All right?'

'You're leaving me here on my own? But it's dark,' Jude said in feigned protest.

The guard laughed, then he opened the door. 'I'll be back,' he said. 'Don't have nightmares.' He left, bolting the door behind him, and Jude heard him trying it several times to make sure it was firmly locked.

He waited until the guard's footsteps had disappeared down the corridor, then clambered up on the shelves again and reached towards the air vent. He saw it move too late; seconds later it clattered to the ground with a crash. Jude stayed stock-still for a minute, hardly daring to breathe, but no one seemed to have heard. Eventually, his heart beginning to slow, Jude hauled himself back up and started to crawl back along the ceiling.

Curiously, Peter opened the envelope he'd been given; seconds later he was still staring at its contents, a mixture of elation and dismay that he didn't entirely understand flooding through him.

'It's Anna's Declaration,' he gasped. 'She's signed it.'

Dr Edwards, who had been discreetly occupying himself with something in the corner ever since the contretemps between Peter and his grandfather that morning, looked up.

'She has?'

Peter looked over at him blankly, waving the

document in his hand. 'She's signed,' he repeated. 'I don't understand. She said . . . I didn't think she . . .'

'So you've got what you wanted?' Dr Edwards asked. 'This is cause for celebration, surely?'

'Yes,' Peter said uncertainly. 'I suppose it is.'

'You don't sound so sure.'

Peter frowned. 'I am. I mean, I'm just not sure why she signed.'

'Perhaps she thought through the alternatives? Didn't the guard say her message was that you were right?'

Peter nodded vaguely. 'I have to go and see her,' he said suddenly. 'I have to see her now.'

'Of course,' Dr Edwards said quickly. 'Are you going to tell your grandfather?'

Carefully returning Anna's Declaration to the envelope and putting it in his pocket, Peter pulled off his lab overall and grabbed his coat. 'You tell him if you want,' he said, then grimaced when he saw Dr Edwards' face fall. 'I didn't mean . . .' he said quickly. 'I just meant, you know, if you see him . . .'

'I know,' Dr Edwards said carefully. 'But you should know I didn't tell him. Before I mean, about you deciding to sign. It wasn't me.'

Peter nodded. 'I know. At least, I guessed. It doesn't matter anyway. Not any more.'

'The next delivery is on its way? Marvellous. That's marvellous, thank you, Eleanor. Pleasure doing business with you.'

Sitting back on his chair, Richard turned to face the window rather than his desk. The sun was throwing vibrant colours into the sky as it made its descent – as he watched it, Richard felt the delicious glow of triumph wash over him. The new House Matron of Grange Hall was proving very amenable. She asked no questions, delivered the goods, and was pretty to boot. Richard couldn't ask for a better business partner. Meanwhile, he was sure now that he could convince Peter to do what was required of him at the conference; afterwards, if he caused problems, Richard would deal with him. Him, the Surplus girl, and that vile little brother of hers.

He closed his eyes, allowing the soft leather of the seat beneath him to soothe his aching muscles, to cocoon him for just a few minutes; a moment of peace before Hillary arrived, before he carried out potentially the most important sales pitch of this half of the century.

But as he opened his eyes, an unfamiliar sight greeted him. Darkness. Low, emergency lighting along the floor.

Immediately he jumped up. 'What is the meaning of this?' he shouted, charging into the corridor like a bull into the ring. 'Where are the lights? Why are these doors open? What's going on?'

A guard approached, his face white and shaken.

'It's a problem with the Energy Centre, sir,' he said nervously.

'Problem? I've got a visitor from the Authorities

arriving any minute,' Richard snapped, taking out his phone and dialling a number. He could feel his face getting red, could feel his heart pounding in his chest. 'Samuels? What the hell is going on?'

'It's the energy system,' Samuels said, the tension audible in his voice. 'It's being rebooted.'

'Rebooted?' Richard asked, his eyes flashing with anger. 'Now is not the time to reboot the system. Stop it. Stop it now.'

'I'm afraid we can't. Seems there's a glitch in the system. A faulty connection. Rebooting it should solve the problem.'

'A glitch?' Richard barked angrily. 'This is Pincent Pharma. We don't have faulty connections. We don't have faulty anything. What is this glitch?'

'I'm afraid I . . . The precise details are currently . . . It's not entirely clear why . . .'

'You don't know?' Richard thundered.

'No, Mr Pincent. But I've got men working on it. Please be reassured that the energy will be restored immediately.'

'If it isn't, you will be sorry,' Richard threatened darkly. 'You and every other person I come across. You will be more sorry than you ever thought possible . . .'

He stopped, staring ahead, wide-eyed. Then he shut off his phone and put it in his pocket.

'Hillary. You're early. You're . . . here.'

'Yes,' she said smoothly, dismissing the guard who had brought her up, with one flick of her hand. 'And no one seemed to mind me waltzing through the lobby and up to your office. Would you like to tell me exactly what's going on?'

Chapter Twenty-one

Peter hadn't been able to get home to see Anna; the blackout had resulted in emergency security measures being imposed and no one was allowed to leave the building. Nor could he reach Anna on the phone; he tried and tried but no one answered. Instead, he and Dr Edwards were left in their lab, twiddling their thumbs, waiting for energy to be restored: all non-essential activity had been shut down, the identi-card system had stopped working, and emergency lighting was on, emitting a low light throughout the building that made each room and corridor feel strange and alien.

'You want to see the drugs being made?' Dr Edwards asked. 'The real hub of production?'

Peter looked up, still preoccupied with thoughts of Anna. 'I thought it was out of bounds,' he said vaguely, remembering his first tour of Pincent Pharma, the peek at the 'finishing area' he was allowed, but no more. 'I thought it took months to secure a pass for the production area.'

Dr Edwards shrugged, his eyes twinkling. 'It does,

usually. But the security system is down, isn't it? Seems like quite a good time to me, bearing in mind your news. And nothing else in the building is working, so there isn't much else to do.'

'OK. Sure. Let me just try Anna one more time.' He dialled the number but no one picked up; a few minutes later, Peter reluctantly followed Dr Edwards out of the lab.

They made their way to the production side of the building, passing through door after door that swung open disconcertingly instead of remaining solidly shut as they usually did. Guards were patrolling the corridors, their expressions grim, but without the identi-card system they didn't know who was meant to be where; whilst Dr Edwards and Peter were stopped several times, they were, each time, allowed to pass freely.

Eventually, they reached the viewing gallery on the fourth floor, the area behind a large glass wall through which Peter could see the small white pills shooting out of funnels. Dr Edwards walked past the window, through a door to his right. 'There,' he said, pointing down the corridor to another glass window. They walked towards it, then Peter gasped. Hundreds of vats sat next to each other, machines hovering over them; into some, powder was being poured, in others, mechanical arms were stirring, large metal lids clamping down over them and lasers beaming down. In front of them large sheets of white lay like undisturbed snow, waiting to be fed into pressing machines, ready for the finishing room. The operation was so much bigger than Peter had expected, so industrial. Those machines, those slabs of white, they were the stuff of eternal life. He shook his head in amazement.

Dr Edwards looked equally entranced. 'Just think, Peter,' he breathed. 'Just think what is contained within those sheets. The perfection of mankind.'

Peter stared at them, wondering how many little spherical pills each would produce. Their pure whiteness made them appear so innocent; their promise of eternal life so irresistible.

'And that's it?' he murmured quietly, transfixed as he watched the pills being born out of large machines. 'You just mix and press? I thought there would be more to it, somehow.'

'There is,' Dr Edwards breathed. 'So much more.' Then his eyes went misty as they stared into the middle distance. 'Sweet Longevity, make me immortal with a kiss,' he whispered.

Peter frowned. 'What?'

'Oh, nothing.' Dr Edwards reddened slightly. 'I was just remembering something . . . another time, another place. You know, it was Albert Fern who got me excited about science in the first place. He was a great scholar. A great lover of human endeavour.'

'Albert Fern?'

'The creator of Longevity. Yes. Your great-grandfather, Peter. He wanted to cure disease, to end suffering. He made me realise what was possible if you never gave up. If you opened your mind to possibility . . .'

'But he died, didn't he? Bit ironic, don't you think?'

Dr Edwards hesitated, then he nodded. 'But the rest of us live, Peter. And he lives on in every tablet, in every human kept alive by them.'

They stood silently, watching the tablets for a few minutes. Then Dr Edwards took off his lab coat. 'Peter, while I'm here I think I might pop upstairs to see the research team. We rarely have the time to discuss our research together these days; I think now might be rather a good opportunity. Can you find your own way back, or do you want me to walk back some of the way?'

Peter shook his head. 'No, I'll be fine. You go.'

'I shouldn't be long,' Dr Edwards said. 'But I'm not sure I'd hang around here if I were you. It is a restricted area.'

He walked down the corridor; Peter barely noticed him go. He was unable to take his eyes away from the Longevity pills, imagining what he could do with the years that stretched out in front of him. He could do anything, go anywhere. The choice was almost paralysing, the decisions endless.

Jude's heart was thudding in his chest and his face was covered in hot, grimy dust. He was back almost where he started – almost but not quite. Below him was the Security Centre, the hub of Pincent Pharma, the source of all information, all the power. He could hear someone swearing beneath him; could hear walkie-talkies going off every few minutes and frantic conversations. Carefully, silently, Jude opened up the box in front of him, the mainframe to the security camera system. His hands were moist with sweat and as he explored the innards of the system the various wires slipped out of his fingers several times, but eventually he found what he was looking for. Silently, he took out his knife and cut two of them, before fusing them together and connecting them to his own mini-com. Its small screen, just six centimetres by ten, flickered into life. Jude held his breath, listening for a sound that might indicate that he'd made a mistake, that the system below him was also was flashing into life, but he was met by silence. Sighing with relief, he moved his fingers to the keypad to the left of the screen and began to search.

'You're sure that Longevity production hasn't been compromised?'

Peter jumped back abruptly at the sound of a high, anxious voice and pressed himself against the wall. Walking towards him, he could see the unmistakable form of his grandfather. A fearsome-looking woman with rigid hair was striding down the corridor next to him.

'Production?' His grandfather's voice sounded

incredulous, but Peter could hear the stress in it. 'Of course it isn't compromised. Non-essential functions are shut down in case of power failure, but never Longevity production. Longevity production and Unit X both have independent back-up energy systems, Hillary. Longevity production never ceases. Really, there's nothing to worry about.'

Peter's eyes widened at the mention of Unit X. It was the place Pip had wanted to know more about, although that seemed almost a lifetime ago now.

'Your security is still down, Richard, which is alarming enough. I thought Pincent Pharma had the most sophisticated systems in the world.'

'It does,' he said grimly. 'And now we know to put it on a grid of its own too. Hillary, people will be fired over this, I can assure you, but it is no reason to be worried. No reason to . . .' He stopped dead as he saw his grandson and stared at him suspiciously. 'Peter! What on earth are you doing here?'

Peter reddened. 'We were . . . me and Dr Edwards, I mean . . . we were looking at the Operations Plant,' he mumbled. 'Dr Edwards had to go and talk to the research team. I was just on my way back.'

His grandfather's eyes narrowed. 'You know that this is a restricted area?'

Peter nodded. 'Dr Edwards said . . .'

'Dr Edwards, I'm sure, knew what he was doing,' his grandfather said tightly, his eyes flickering over to the woman. 'But perhaps you should return to your workstation, Peter. As quickly as possible.'

'So this is Peter Pincent. How very interesting.' The woman was staring at Peter curiously.

Peter said nothing. He wanted to ask about Unit X, wanted to reassure himself that it was just another unit, that there was a perfectly reasonable explanation to quash the doubts now nagging at him.

'Yes, yes it is,' his grandfather said, his eyes still trained on Peter suspiciously. 'Hillary, this is Peter. Peter, Hillary Wright is the Deputy Secretary General at the Authorities.'

Peter surveyed the woman quickly. Her eyes were narrow, her posture upright.

'So, I hear you are a convert to Longevity.'

'I . . .' Peter dug his nails into his palms. 'I think Longevity is an incredible thing,' he said carefully.

'And you'll be signing the Declaration at the press conference this afternoon?' Hillary continued, her eyes fixed on him beadily.

Peter balked slightly. 'Press conference? I'm not very good with press –' he said.

'They are a necessary evil, I'm afraid,' Hillary said sharply. 'People will be curious, Peter. You're rather famous, you know.'

'I thought I was more infamous,' Peter said.

'Fame, infamy, they're of the same family,' Hillary said, smiling thinly. 'I think it would be a good idea.'

She shot a look at Peter's grandfather, whose expression was unreadable. 'I'm sure Peter will agree,' he said, his voice low. 'Signing the Declaration is something to celebrate, after all.'

Peter looked back uncomfortably. He might be signing the Declaration, but that didn't make him a puppet for the Authorities, for Pincent Pharma.

'No,' he said. 'No, I don't think I . . .' Then he hesitated. Perhaps a press conference might not be such a bad idea. It would serve the Underground right, after all. It would show Pip once and for all that Peter was his own man. It would show that he couldn't be manipulated any more, couldn't be used.

'Actually, why not?' he said eventually.

'Good,' Hillary said. 'I know that Richard will ensure that you're briefed.'

'Of course,' his grandfather said cautiously. '6 p.m., Peter. Now, I think you'd better go back to your lab.'

Peter made his way to the other end of the corridor where he turned left. They thought they were using him, but they weren't; he was using them, he thought to himself, swaggering slightly. No one used Peter. Not any more. But then he stopped. Something was gnawing at his stomach. Something wasn't right. Maybe he'd been a little hasty. He hadn't even spoken to Anna yet. Her signed Declaration was burning a hole in his pocket and he needed to know more than anything why she'd changed her mind.

Quickly, he turned and he started to retrace his steps. He would tell his grandfather that he needed more time. He would insist that when he chose to sign the Declaration was his own business. But as he turned the corner, he stopped abruptly. His grandfather had disappeared. He ran ahead to the end of the corridor, but when he looked left and right there was no sign of them.

Annoyed, Peter continued to look around, trying to listen out for the sound of their footsteps, but eventually he had to accept defeat. They had, it seemed, disappeared into thin air.

Chapter Twenty-two

Anna watched the guard silently, her eyes wide with dread and fear. She'd been dragged out of Maria's apartment and thrown in the back of a van; thankfully she'd got Ben back and had been able to persuade the men to take her handcuffs off so that she could cradle him in her arms and shield him from the walls of the van as it careered down the road. Now she was in a darkened room; she didn't know where it was. The van had pulled up outside a door; the door had led to a corridor; the corridor had led to this room.

'If you don't shut that thing up, I will,' snapped the guard.

She pulled Ben towards her and tried to soothe him; he'd been crying since they arrived.

'He's hungry,' she said quietly. 'He needs some milk.'

'He needs some milk,' the guard mocked. 'Just shut him up, or he'll get more than milk.'

Anna felt her stomach clench with fear and she quickly put Ben's thumb in his mouth, which he sucked violently. The lights in the room were dim, disorienting.

'Where's Maria?' she asked tentatively. 'Is she here too?'

The guard grinned. 'Maria?' he asked. 'Coming here? I doubt it. Maria's a Catcher.'

Anna went white. 'No,' she said desperately. 'She can't . . . She said . . .'

'I'm afraid you can't trust everthing that people say,' a voice said as the door opened and another man walked into the room. He was thin-faced, wearing a suit; an air of menace surrounded him.

'Anna Covey?' he asked.

She nodded.

'My name is Mr Samuels. I'm Head of Security here at Pincent Pharma. And I'm afraid, Anna, that you've got yourself into a spot of bother. We have everything on film, you see.'

Anna could barely breathe. 'Everything?'

'Everything.' Mr Samuels smiled nastily. 'You were heard plotting to free Surpluses, Anna. Do you know what sentence that crime carries?'

Anna shook her head.

'I just wanted to help the children,' she said, tears pricking at her eyes. 'I thought she wanted to help, too. I thought . . .'

'Enough!' Mr Samuels barked. 'You think we're going to stand by and allow some upstart Surplus to plot against our society, to threaten science and civilisation? We have to protect the rest of society from people like you, Anna. You and that disgusting baby brother of yours don't deserve to live on the Outside, do you?'

'Not Ben,' Anna said, her voice quivering. 'This has nothing to do with him. He's Legal. He's innocent.'

'Innocent? Who's going to look after him if you're in prison, Anna? Didn't think of that, did you? Too busy thinking about those dirty Surpluses.'

Anna felt the blood drain from her face, the dreadful realisation of what she'd done thudding in her head like an avalanche of pain. A buzzing sound emanated from Mr Samuel's pocket and he pulled out a walkie-talkie.

'I do not want to be disturbed. Do you understand?' he said, his voice low and irritable. 'I want two units guarding the main entrance and I want the blackout fixed and unless the four horsemen of the Apocalypse are seen approaching the building, I don't want any further interruptions, do you understand? Good.'

He put the device in his pocket and smiled thinly at Anna. 'Now we'll just wait for the doctor, shall we?' he said. 'Got to give you a medical. See how Useful you're going to be.'

'Useful?' Anna's voice was thin, barely audible. 'What's going to happen to me? Where am I going?'

But Mr Samuels didn't let her finish; instead, Ben was snatched from her by a guard and Anna was thrust on to the bed before Ben was handed back to her. He was screaming now, his hands drawn into tiny fists, tears cascading down his red, swollen cheeks and it was all Anna could do not to join him.

The world came into focus slowly. White ceiling. White pillow. Red blanket. Greyish sheets. Surplus Sheila lay silently, looking around her cautiously as she gradually remembered where she was. Not in Grange Hall – that much she knew. But not a house, either. It was an interim place, she'd decided, for her medical. Sheila knew better than to ask questions, though; she'd learnt in her years at Grange Hall all about keeping her eyes cast downwards, asking no questions, obeying orders, even if she'd fought against it. This was probably just another test, she told herself, just to check that she was fit and ready to be a housekeeper. If she passed, she would soon be out in the real world, in a real house. And once she was in a house, she'd go about finding her parents.

Allowing a little smile on to her face, Sheila looked around. Her brain felt fuzzy, her limbs heavy on the thin mattress beneath her. She vaguely remembered arriving here, remembered being driven up towards a large, white building. She'd been scared when she got out of the white van, had asked where she was, but they hadn't told her, and when a man had dragged her towards a door, she'd started to shout and someone else had stuck something sharp in her leg. She couldn't remember anything after that. And now she was here in another dormitory, just like Grange Hall but white, not grey, and there were no bells, no chores, no Training. She'd been here a few days, she thought. Maybe longer – she kept falling asleep and it was hard to keep track.

There were others in the room, others like her, on beds, all girls, all asleep or feigning sleep. She caught a girl's eye and they both looked away quickly. One of the girls had been caught trying to start a conversation a day or so before and had been punished for it with a beating; Sheila had thought it served her right for being Stupid; hoped that they would notice that she wasn't breaking any rules, that she should pass the test more quickly than the other girls.

The tests weren't very nice. Sheila had decided that she didn't like medicals very much at all. Every day she was given an injection; every day they took blood from her; every day her legs were hoisted into stirrups and metal instruments prodded inside her painfully as she clamped her mouth shut and did her best not to cry out in pain. But apart from that, she was left almost entirely alone. There was a small, cramped bathroom, which the girls were allowed to visit, one at a time. Three times a day a tray of food was placed in front of her. All the girls were wearing the same gowns – long at the front, open at the back, which meant they had to hold the two sides together firmly whenever they made their way to the bathroom. And every so often, one of the girls would be replaced with a new face; they'd passed their tests, Sheila thought enviously. They'd been allowed out, to become housekeepers. She hoped that she'd be next. She couldn't wait.

Jude flicked from camera to camera, searching for the girl, for Peter. Instead, his screen was filled with shots of laboratories, production lines, the cafeteria, long sweeping corridors, the reception hall. At the sight of this screen, Jude paused – a line of guards were now positioned outside the glass doors, armed and ready for action; a further three were positioned inside. Jude recognised one of them as the guard who had been assigned to him.

A man was being searched by the guards; moments later, he emerged through the doors and headed towards the reception desk. Jude watched silently. The man was holding up an identi-card; Judge zoomed in and saw the words 'Manchester Evening News' written on it and the name 'WILLIAM ANDERSON'. The guard took it and scrutinised it, then seemed to be demanding something else; the man in the suit shrugged, smiling, then took out a piece of paper and handed it to him. The guard appeared satisfied; he was soon standing up and showing the man into a side room off the lobby. It was only as they passed the camera outside the door that Jude saw the man's face properly for the first time, saw his eyes. Jude felt a trickle of sweat wend its way down his neck. The man wasn't a journalist. He wasn't from Manchester. And he wasn't called William Anderson. Shaking slightly, he stared at the screen as the man disappeared from view.

Chapter Twenty-three

The corridor stretched out, long, white and brightly lit, and Peter looked around it curiously. It was, he'd established, on the outer perimeter of the main building; from the windows on the right-hand side the whole of Pincent Pharma could be seen – its buildings within buildings, its outside spaces, its long tunnel-like corridors, which circled it like snakes.

It was a wide corridor, with installations at various intervals – at one end there were display stands showing the ascent of man; at the other end were several more explaining an aspect of the Longevity production process. There were two identi-card stands where passers-by could check their blood pressure, nutritional levels, brain activity and antibody presence. Two large cabinets against the wall revealed within them life-size models of the human body, clearly displaying the position and look of each human organ, each bone and ligament. One of the models was 'healthy' or, rather, post-Longevity; the other showed a body that had aged, its organs failing, its muscles wasted, its skeleton drooping.

Peter wasn't interested in the models, though. Instead, he moved back to the wall and leant against it. His logical brain told him to go back to the lab, to find his grandfather later. But something in his bones wouldn't let him. Deep down inside he knew something wasn't right. Sighing, he peeled himself off the wall. Unit X. It was on the sixth floor, Pip had said; Peter was on the fourth. He looked up at the ceiling searchingly, looking for his own peace of mind as much as anything else, and then he frowned; behind him, he could hear voices. The sound was very muffled, but there was no doubt in Peter's mind. This was no engine humming; it was the sound of voices. Human voices.

Confused, Peter looked around, but there was no explanation for the sound. Had he been mistaken? Was he going mad? But then, he heard a voice again, and not just any voice. It was the voice of his grandfather. It was muffled, but there was no mistaking it.

Slowly, he turned round to look properly at the model next to him. And then he noticed something, something behind it – a panel with edges.

Frowning, he manoeuvred himself behind the casement, his fingers searching the wall, feeling around the panel for a catch, for something indicating that the panel could move, could open. He was so close; he knew he was, and yet his tugs, his pulls, yielded nothing. Sighing, he stepped back to check he wasn't missing anything, then, frustrated, he leant against the panel. Immediately, it clicked open, and Peter stared in disbelief as it swung open, revealing a steep staircase leading upwards. Quickly, Peter checked that the corridor was still empty, then, holding his breath, and making sure to close the panel behind him, he began to climb.

Richard took out his phone. 'Yes?' he barked.

'Richard, it's Derek Samuels. The doctor's just left.'

Richard's eyes flickered over to Hillary then back again. 'Ah, Samuels. I'm . . . I'm with someone at the moment. Can this wait?'

'I don't think so. You're not going to believe this.'

'Believe what, exactly?' he said, not attempting to hide the annoyance in his voice. 'I hope there's nothing wrong.'

'Nothing's wrong, Richard. She's pregnant. The doctor said just over three months.'

Richard's mouth fell open.

'Richard? Did you hear what I said?'

Richard nodded; he could see Hillary was straining to listen. 'Yes,' he said quickly. 'Yes, I'm just with someone, that's all . . . What you were saying, that's . . . that's interesting.' He shot her a smile. 'Excuse me just one minute,' he said, then walked around the corner, out of earshot.

'Who knows about this?' he hissed into the phone a few seconds later.

'No one.'

'Good. Keep it that way.'

Samuels paused. 'So what do you want to do?

About the foetus?'

'Give it to Dr Ferguson to do as he pleases.'

'You mean it? What about the father?'

'I don't believe there is one,' Richard Pincent said evenly.

'No father?'

'No.'

'Of course,' Samuels said quickly. 'No father.' Richard could hear the surprise in his voice, and it irked him.

'A live foetus is gold dust, isn't it?' Richard asked impatiently. 'Isn't Ferguson always crying out for live cells to experiment on?'

'Yes, sir. Yes, I believe he is.'

'Then get on with it,' he hissed. 'I'm with a senior representative from the Authorities. I have a press conference today and a blackout to contend with. I don't want to be bothered with anything else, do you understand?'

'Completely,' Samuels said quickly. 'Consider it dealt with.'

Chapter Twenty-four

Shivering under the thin blankets, Sheila rolled over on to her side. Her stomach was swollen and sensitive to the touch and she wriggled awkwardly to get comfortable, then slowly allowed her eyes to close and tried to coax her body into sleep.

She was woken what felt like minutes later by the sound of voices close by. Sheila froze. Voices close by were never a good thing in her experience of this place.

'Right. So we think this one's nearly ready?'

'Levels look right.'

'Lovely. And how many are we looking at?'

'At least twelve, maybe more.'

The other voice whistled. 'Great. OK, then, let's wheel her in.'

Sheila felt her bed moving and she opened her eyes, fearfully. Behind her was a heavy-set man, pushing her bed; at the foot, pulling her, was a nurse she recognised.

'Where . . . where am I going?' she asked, trying to keep her voice level.

The nurse looked at her irritably. 'Does it matter?'

'Am I going back to Grange Hall?'

The nurse grimaced. 'No, Surplus. You're about to repay your debt to society, young woman.'

'Does that mean I'm going to be a housekeeper now?' Sheila asked hopefully. 'Does that mean I'm going to a house?'

The nurse laughed. 'A house? Give me a break. Now shut up or I'll have to inject you, and the doctor prefers you lot awake, understand?'

'Awake?' Sheila asked, before she could stop herself. 'For what? What's the doctor going to do to me?'

'What's the doctor going to do to me?' the nurse repeated, her voice mocking. Then she looked past Sheila to the orderly pushing her bed. 'All right, stop a second will you?'

The bed stopped and the nurse pulled out a needle. 'Just a little one,' she said. 'She'll be awake in time for the op.'

Sheila felt a hand clamping hold of her arm and the sharp pain of a needle being inserted into it.

'That's better,' the nurse said to no one in particular as she disposed of the needle. 'You'd have thought with all the experiments they do on Surpluses they'd have mutated a gene by now to stop them talking. Organ regrowth is all very well, but what about us? We're the ones that have to deal with them day in, day out.'

Sheila's head started to spin and, seconds later, she

felt herself falling into a deep sleep.

The room Peter found himself in reminded him of the old depots and derelict warehouses he'd spent time in when he was younger, being dropped off, picked up, left sometimes for days at a time while the Underground tried to work out what to do with him, tried to find someone who'd be prepared to take him in. Boys were difficult, Pip would mutter to him; girls were easier to hide, easier to entertain. Boys needed space to run around, but running around simply wasn't an option for illicit children, not with prying eyes everywhere, not with the Catchers ready to pounce at any minute. It had got harder as he had got older, too – there were always homes for young children, always people who would offer to hide babies, but a growing boy was a challenge. Any boy more than five years old was difficult to place.

Peter frowned and pushed the memory from his mind. Then, pausing only briefly to take in the shabby state of the room, the boxes piled up, the unswept concrete floor, he scanned the room. In the far corner, only just visible behind a pile of what looked like rubbish and rubble, he saw a door. Checking that there was no one to see him, he scurried towards it and opened it just a fraction. The first thing he heard on opening the door was the voice of his grandfather, and he quickly jumped back.

'So you see,' his grandfather was saying, 'Longevity is a wonder drug, but it has its limitations. What we're developing here is the next stage. Longevity 5.4. Or, for marketing purposes, Longevity+.' They were walking towards a staircase; Peter strained to listen.

Hillary shrugged. 'If you say so. Now, can we get on with this? The Authorities have other pressing concerns, Richard. Concerns that rather supersede Longevity.'

Peter's grandfather smiled thinly. 'Supersede Longevity? Hillary, nothing supersedes Longevity. Nothing ever will. If Longevity production were to cease, the human race would die out in a matter of years. Civilisation as we know it would crumble. The human race is now entirely dependent on Longevity for its very survival.'

There was silence for a few seconds.

'Very well, Richard, you've made your point.'

'Good. And now, if you'll just follow me into Unit X, I will show you the future.'

Peter waited for them to reach the top of the stairs, then silently slipped through the door he was hiding behind and followed them.

Sheila squinted against the bright light that was shining into her eyes. Her arm was aching where the nurse had stuck a needle into her, and her head was feeling woozy, as though she was still in a dream, and it gave her confidence, encouraged her to open her mouth.

'Where am I?' she asked no one in particular, trying to focus her blurred vision and failing miserably. She could see that she was in a large room; she could hear low voices, but couldn't see who was speaking. 'What's happening?'

The blurry outline of a woman wandered over to her side. When she was close, Sheila could see her face. It looked kind, so different from the people who'd been manhandling her for the past week or so.

'Surplus Sheila?' she asked. Sheila nodded. 'Welcome to Unit X,' the woman continued. 'Your procedure will be starting soon. It's relatively painless, and you need to stay as still as possible. Can you do that for me?'

Sheila nodded. 'The procedure,' she said. 'What's it for?'

The woman smiled. 'It's for making history,' she said. 'You're going to be helping us with a scientific breakthrough, Sheila. You're about to become a Valuable Asset.'

'Really?' Sheila felt herself bristle with something approaching pride. She was going to make history. She was important. Then she winced. 'It hurts,' she said. 'It really hurts. And I feel sick.'

'You'll be fine,' the woman said. 'I'll be back very soon. Just lie there quietly, will you? And don't worry, everything will be OK.'

She disappeared out of view, and Sheila put her hands on her stomach, wishing the pain would subside but knowing there would be no point in making a fuss. She felt her face getting hot under the lights, and tried to roll on to her side but her legs were clamped in a strange position. Her arms, too, were restrained, she discovered when she tried to move them.

Anxiously, she called after the woman, but there was no response.

Peter took the steps two at a time; at the top was a short corridor, at the end of which was another door. Unit X, he found himself thinking, his heart thudding in his chest. This was it. Pressing his ear against the door, he listened.

'The problem with Longevity is not what it can do; it's what it can't do, wouldn't you say?' he heard his grandfather say. 'Our age shouldn't be visible, shouldn't have any impact whatsoever on our bodies, but it does, doesn't it? Our wrinkles, our spare tyres, our lack of energy – they conspire against us. Nature is still laughing at us, holding us back. We have inherited the earth, and yet we cannot control how we feel, how we look.'

'There's always surgery.'

They were close to the door – too close for Peter to risk opening it.

'Yes, but surgery is only a sticking-plaster. One operation is never enough, Hillary; we are permanent fixtures in this world. Our internal organs are Renewing themselves constantly with the help of Longevity, but our skin, our muscles, have yet to catch up.'

'And you can help them? Really? How?'

'Stem cells.'

Peter heard Hillary sigh. 'Stem cells? Richard, what's new about that?' There was a screaming noise that made Peter jump with alarm. 'And what's all that noise? Do you have animals up here?'

'Animals? No. That's just . . . part of the process. The important thing to remember here is that we're not dealing with animal stem cells, or stem cells taken from adults, Hillary. Adult stem cells are so limited. Once they've developed beyond a certain point, they can only repair, replace or be grown into specific organs.'

'So? What's the alternative?'

'It's in this room, Hillary. Just beyond those double doors.'

'Then show me what's behind them, Richard. I want to see.'

Peter gritted his teeth with frustration. He needed to get in, needed to see for himself.

'And you will. We have within our grasp the Holy Grail of anti-ageing, if you'll just wash your hands over there and put on this gown . . .'

'But I don't understand. I don't . . .'

'You will! We're already at the testing stage. Unofficially, that is. But so far, there's been nothing but an increase in demand from our . . . the participants in our trials.' He grinned. 'I promise you, Hillary, this is going to be absolutely huge. For us, for the nation . . . Follow me, and prepare to be amazed.'

*

Sheila moaned softly, and tried in vain to free her arms. She didn't feel important any more; she felt unhappy, afraid, uncomfortable. She could hear screams every so often, and it scared her.

A man appeared in a white coat, walking briskly towards her. Next to him was the nice woman who was organising things on a trolley. Sheila's vision was improving gradually; she could make out other beds, people in white coats talking in hushed voices.

'OK, number please?'

'Let's see now . . . She's VA 367.' The woman didn't smile at Sheila this time; she just walked over, and pressed a lever which raised Sheila's legs up into the air, wrenching her down the bed so that she grazed her wrists on the manacles.

'And the number for the retrieval?'

'Oh, twelve.'

'Twelve?' The man sounded impressed. 'Not bad. That's the record so far, isn't it?'

The woman nodded. 'We had an unsuccessful eleven last week.'

'Right, well, let's make sure this is successful then, shall we?'

He adjusted the light so that it was shining between Sheila's legs and pulled up her gown. She was hot and embarrassed, but was unable to move.

'It hurts,' she managed to say to the woman, who had in her hands several small glass tubes. The woman smiled.

'No, it doesn't,' she said brightly. 'This really isn't

that difficult. Just lie still and let the technician get on with the procedure. It will be over soon.'

Sheila nodded obediently. And then, as she felt something cold and hard jabbing inside her, a blood-curdling scream filled the room. Sheila only realised a few seconds later that she was making the noise herself. The pain was excruciating, like a knife tearing through her. But it was more than pain. Somewhere, deep inside, her body was crying for something and Sheila didn't know why or what, but it felt like her cries came from the deepest part of her soul.

She tried to protest, but the pain shooting through her abdomen made it impossible. Instead, she felt her eyes well up with tears and she prayed that whatever was happening would be over soon, because she knew she couldn't endure it for much longer. She didn't want to be a Valuable Asset any more. She just wanted to be Surplus Sheila.

Chapter Twenty-five

Peter heard his grandfather open another door; he waited for a few seconds, then, tentatively, opened the door he'd been crouching behind. As he crept through, he saw a flash of white light as his grandfather and Hillary disappeared through two double doors. He found himself in an antechamber; on a counter in front of him was a large sink with gowns hanging next to it and a shelf with small plastic bags on it, which, on closer inspection, turned out to contain latex gloves. Quickly, Peter made his way towards the double doors and pushed at one a fraction so he could see into the room; immediately, his eyes opened wide in shock. The room was very large; along the farthest end were five beds, all with girls in them. As he looked at them, he felt a slight nausea rising up inside of him. Their faces were pale, their eyes glassy or closed. Two of them had their legs in the air, held by strange metal contraptions, which Peter found it hard to look at. The girls all looked his age, younger even. Around one were men and women in white coats. At Peter's end of the room were various machines and three empty beds stacked on top of each other; Peter made sure no one was looking, then ran to the beds and hid behind them.

From this vantage point, he saw his grandfather turn to Hillary, a smile on his face. 'The Surplus,' he said easily. 'A drain on society. A burden that the planet can't cope with. Right?'

Hillary shot an uncomfortable look in the girls' direction, then looked away quickly. 'These are Surpluses? Why are they here?'

'My question, Hillary. Answer my question, please.'

Hillary sighed. 'They have their uses, some of them. But yes, overall, they are a drain. Richard, why am I here? I want to see the drugs, not these girls.'

'You are here because the Authorities must sanction the means as well as the end,' Richard said smoothly. 'Sanction and protect our production lines from prying eyes, from questions, from people who don't understand science, who don't realise that every move forward in science requires a . . . a freedom not afforded all disciplines.'

'Freedom? What do you mean?' Hillary asked.

'What if I was to tell you that Surpluses were the key to the health and wellbeing of mankind?' Richard said. 'What if I was to tell you that Surpluses are not a burden, but our saviours? That they are, in fact, not Surpluses at all, but Valuable Assets?'

Peter strained to listen, scanning the room for a closer hiding place.

'Our saviours? Richard, what are you talking about?'

'We have been so short-sighted, Hillary. We have been viewing Surpluses all wrong – as a burden, as something to be avoided, destroyed, managed. But they're not a burden. They are our future. Their eggs, their sperm, their organs, their wombs . . . all more valuable than any other natural resource,' Richard said softly, turning to look at the girls in the beds. As he did so, Peter made a dash for the bench in the centre of the room and crouched down, all his reflexes on full alert.

'Wombs?' Hillary said uncertainly. 'What's so great about their wombs? Richard, you are making no sense. Fertility is a weakness. Creating new life is a sin.'

Peter's grandfather licked his lips and gestured towards the row of beds.

'Think of them as incubators. Incubators that can grow state-of-the-art embryonic stem cells,' he said reverently.

'Embryonic? You mean . . .'

'I mean, embryos. Ten at a time. We're hoping to get up to twelve today. Eventually the sky's the limit.'

'And you're making them? Here?' Hillary gasped.

'It's not that radical, Hillary. Remember IVF, or was that before your time? You take an egg, you fertilise it, you put it in the womb. Only we do four, five, ten, twenty. We let them take hold, let them grow, then we harvest them – and the cells, Hillary, the cells can do anything. Take a precursor stem cell and subject it to the Longevity formula, and the results are . . . well, they're beautiful. Astounding. Revolutionary. Two weeks is all it takes, Hillary. Two weeks from fertilisation.'

Hillary looked up at him in wonderment.

'But the supply,' she said, her forehead wrinkled in concentration. 'The supply's not high enough. Not to supply the country, let alone the world. There aren't enough Surpluses. It's not sustainable.'

Peter's grandfather laughed. 'Of course it's sustainable. We just have to make sure we control the supply.'

'But how? There's no guarantee . . .'

'No guarantee?' Peter's grandfather smiled, and shook his head. Then he lowered his voice. 'You and the Authorities know full well that Surpluses have been used for new ingredients for years – blood donation, bone marrow, stem cells. We've always needed a certain level of supply of Surpluses for medical research, and certain departments within the Authorities have been most . . . sympathetic. But until now, it's been low level – a few faulty birth-control implants here and there ensured an adequate supply. All I'm saying now is that we need to crank it up. We need more young flesh, more Valuable Assets. Officially.'

Peter felt himself go numb as he remembered the comings and goings of strange doctors at Grange Hall, always at night-time, always in Solitary, the underground cells used for punishment, and it was all he could do to breathe in and out. There was nothing pure about Longevity.

'The Authorities . . . you mean, we sanctioned the creation of Surpluses?' Hillary's mouth was open in shock.

'You didn't know?' Peter's grandfather asked, his tone surprised. 'I thought you'd read Adrian's notes. He gave us special dispensation. And now we need to plant more. We need large numbers. Surplus farms. They are our lifeblood, Hillary. The potential is unending.'

Hillary couldn't seem to take her eyes off the girls. 'There are channels, Richard. You'd be breaking protocols and regulations . . .'

'Protocols and regulations that will be swept aside when people understand what the drugs can do. Protocols and regulations that are outdated, that belong to another time. This is progress. This is the future.'

Hillary was silent for a few moments, then she looked back at the row of beds.

'This girl here,' she said, pointing to the girl clamped to the bed. 'What's happening to her?'

'Ah, well, she's at the most exciting stage of the process. Our first twelve, I believe. Twelve embryos, about two weeks old, are being extracted. Twelve embryos with enough stem cells to provide London and the Home Counties with Longevity+ for three months.'

'You mean she's pregnant?'

'Pregnant as a sow,' he confirmed. 'Unfortunately we've yet to bypass the side effects of pregnancy.' He grinned at Hillary. 'Nothing like a ward full of girls feeling sick, tired, wailing and getting upset over nothing to get the nurses demanding pay rises. Still, we're working on it. If it didn't compromise the quality of the embryos, we'd keep them unconscious all the way through.'

'And what will happen to her . . . afterwards?'

'Afterwards?' Richard looked at her uncertainly.

'Will she blab? We can't have the girls talking.' Peter felt a chill inside him; even from where he was hiding he could see the steely glint in Hillary's eye. Any hope that she might be outraged by what she was seeing was immediately dashed.

'Oh, I see,' Richard said, looking relieved. 'No, she won't be able to blab. To start with, each girl has a good fifteen years of production ahead of her, I'd say. After that, who knows.'

'Who knows? Richard, don't give me platitudes. What will happen to the girls when they are no longer Valuable? We can't keep creating Surpluses if they're going to become Burdens later on.'

'Burdens? Oh, they won't be Burdens,' Richard said, smiling lightly. 'They'll just become Valuable in other ways. We need live bodies for experiments, to test our drugs, so that's one possibility. Organs are still needed to hone our organ-growth techniques; blood is also an important resource. There are many wonderful things to be harvested from the human body, Hillary. The possibilities are endless.'

'It's incredible,' Hillary breathed. 'Who'd have thought Surpluses could be so useful?'

Slowly, Peter allowed his eyes to travel to where the girl lay. He felt numb, felt like his skin was too tight on his body, too close. He'd actually thought that Longevity was beautiful. But there was nothing good about Pincent Pharma. It was evil. More evil than he'd ever imagined, and he felt sick at the thought that he'd come so close to signing up to its cause.

He had to get out, he realised. He had to tell Pip, had to get help. Tentatively, he began to stand up, rubbing his legs, which felt stiff from crouching, and looking for his opportunity to run to the door, hoping that everyone's attention would be on the girl at the end of the row, the girl who was being operated on. Aghast, he stared as a man in a lab coat thrust a metal implement inside her. The girl let out another blood-curdling scream, disturbing the man carrying out the operation.

'I think we'll have to sedate this one,' the doctor said. 'Inject her. Do it quickly.'

The girl lifted her head and continued to scream, a sound that came from the depths of despair, a guttural cry for help. And then Peter realised she was looking over at him, and he frowned, because he knew her. It was Surplus Sheila, from Grange Hall, and she'd seen him.

'Surplus Peter!' she screamed, just before the nurse

stuck a needle into her arm. 'Peter. Help me. Please . . .'

Peter ducked down, but it was too late. His grandfather swung round and scanned the room wildly.

Hillary looked around anxiously. 'Surplus Peter? Not Surplus P— Not your . . .'

'Peter,' said his grandfather slowly, 'if you are in here, you are going to wish with all your heart that you were not.' Then he took out his phone and dialled a number. 'It's me,' he barked. 'I need armed guards in Unit X. Right away.'

Chapter Twenty-six

Jude had lost Pip. He had passed straight by the Security Centre, through the door at the end of the corridor, and Jude hadn't been able to find the relevant camera view. His breathing was returning to normal, though; at first, he'd found himself worrying that perhaps Pip had come for him, that his warning not to fly too close to the sun was a serious one. But then he'd kicked himself; Pip had no reason to follow Jude around. He'd have far bigger fish to fry. But what were they? Had he come for Peter?

Jude returned to his search, anxiously, flicking through the camera system. It took him a while, but eventually he found her. His princess. His red-haired beauty.

A red-haired Surplus, he suddenly realised, noticing the Embedded Time on her fragile wrist. He'd been brought up to despise Surpluses, to see them as vermin, a threat to civilisation, a threat to Legal people like him. But then he'd found out how close he had come to being Surplus himself; it was because of Jude that Peter had been a Surplus. His tutor had once told him about the old religion called Christianity, about the concept of Original Sin – a barbaric idea, his tutor had scoffed. But Jude understood Original Sin perfectly. Lately he'd begun to think it summed him up.

He stared at the girl, wondering what her own story was, imagining what it would be like to talk to her, to have her listen to him, to share their stories and their dreams. Why was she there, he wondered? Was she ill? Perhaps he could take care of her. Perhaps she could take care of him too.

Not taking his eyes off her, he pressed a button to zoom in. But as her face filled the screen, he realised with a jolt that she was awake. Her eyes seemed to be staring right at him – beautiful, expressive eyes that looked terrified, dark with horror. As he felt his muscles tighten, he trained the camera back to see what was causing her distress, to understand the tears in her eyes. There were doctors and nurses round her, doing things to her – things that made Jude shudder. And then he felt a prickle at the back of his neck as he saw three other figures. He recognised the man immediately – it was Richard Pincent, the man whose face was plastered on every piece of Longevity advertising, who was regularly on the news, in the papers. There was a woman too; he didn't recognise her. But he did recognise Peter. Recognised those darting eyes, those clenched fists. The girl was screaming now, her mouth wide open, her face red with anger; her legs, he could see now, were in some sort of strange manacles.

'Up there. He's in the ceiling.' Jude started slightly; the voice came from below, in the Security Centre. He could hear a ladder being dragged along the floor. Any minute now, the air vent a few feet away from him would open up and he'd be caught.

Desperately, his eyes glued to the tiny screen, Jude forced himself to disconnect it from the mainframe and the image of the girl disappeared. He shoved his mini-com back in his pocket, took a deep breath and crawled as quickly as he could towards the lift shaft.

Peter had come out of his hiding place immediately, his eyes fixed on his grandfather; there was no point in doing anything else. 'What are you doing to Sheila?' he seethed. He wasn't scared; he was angry, white with hatred, bitterness coursing through his veins. His voice was low, measured. He would not allow his anger to weaken him in any way. 'What's happening to her?'

Richard Pincent stared at him; he was shaking with rage.

'How? How did you get here? No one knows. No one . . .'

'I followed you. It wasn't exactly hard.'

'You followed us?' He walked over to Peter and grabbed him by the shoulders. 'You followed us? How dare you? You cheap little spy.'

Peter shook him off; Richard grabbed him again, this time with more force.

'What are you going to do with him?' Hillary asked anxiously. 'What if he tells someone what he's seen?'

'He won't tell anyone anything,' Richard said darkly. 'The guards will be here any moment; they'll see to that.'

''You going to chain me up, too?' Peter asked, through gritted teeth. 'Turn me into a Useful resource? You make me sick. You *are* sick. Sick in the head.'

'Enough!' His grandfather swung a blow at him, catching him on the head and knocking him to the floor.

Peter pulled himself up, his face defiant, and looked at Hillary. 'And you condone this? The Authorities are happy, are they?'

Hillary looked at him uncomfortably. 'All Pincent Pharma's processes will continue to be reviewed and checked by an appropriate department,' she said, moving away from Peter apprehensively. 'Naturally there are standards and we need to ensure that we are meeting our aims and objectives . . .'

'Objectives,' Peter said. 'Of course. Got to meet those, haven't you?'

As he spoke, the door opened and two guards appeared.

'What took you so long?' Richard asked angrily, motioning for them to grab Peter; they ran towards him and handcuffed his hands behind his back.

One of the guards looked up. 'Yes, sir. Sorry, sir. It's the power cut. Looks like it was sabotage, not a system failure. We're heightening security.'

'Sabotage? You mean the Underground?' Hillary asked fretfully.

Richard turned to Peter. 'Have you got anything to do with this?' he asked icily.

Peter shook his head. 'I wish I did,' he muttered.

'Take him,' Richard said to the guards. 'Lock him up downstairs in one of the storerooms behind reception.'

They pulled Peter towards the door; as he tried to break free, one of them hit him around the head.

'Wait!' Hillary called out, halting the guards in their tracks. 'The press conference. We need him to appear at the press conference.'

'Don't worry,' Richard said tightly. 'He'll sign as arranged.'

Peter shot him a look of disgust. 'You think I'm going to sign the Declaration now? Not in a million years. I'm glad the Underground sabotaged your energy supply. I hope they blow this place up.'

'Of course you'll sign,' Richard said. 'And you'll smile for the journalists, too. After all, if you don't, your little friend Anna will pay the consequences.'

'Anna?' Peter glared at him. 'You leave Anna out of this.'

'I wish I could,' his grandfather said, his expression suggesting the opposite. 'But it appears Anna has been a foolish girl. She's been getting involved in seditious activity behind your back.'

'What?' Peter said uncertainly. 'You're lying.'

'Lying? I wouldn't dream of it. We've got the evidence on tape – the girl provided plans of Grange Hall for some sort of break-in. What was she thinking?' His grandfather shook his head and Peter felt himself go white.

'She was planning to break into a Surplus Hall? With whom? Richard, this is a serious business,' Hillary interjected.

'With no one,' he reassured her. 'It was a set-up. Her contact was a Catcher.'

'A Catcher?' Peter stared at his grandfather in disbelief. 'You set her up? You bastard. You . . .'

'Insurance, Peter. Insurance,' Richard smiled. 'You don't think I would rely on you to do the right thing, do you?'

'Where is she?' Peter demanded. 'What have you done with her?'

'She's perfectly safe, Peter,' his grandfather replied icily. 'But unless you sign the Declaration at 6 p.m. this evening, smiling for the journalists' photographs, I can't guarantee that she'll remain so for much longer.'

Constrained by the guards, Peter twisted to look back at the girls, back at Sheila.

'The Surplus Sterilisation Programme,' Peter said, suddenly, his voice tight. 'Sheila's name was on the list. How can she be pregnant if she was sterilised?'

'Surplus Sterilisation Programme? But it never got ratified,' Hillary said, surprised. 'It was only ever a discussion paper . . .' Her voice trailed off as she saw the look on Peter's face.

'You . . .' His face contorted with confusion then anger as the truth dawned on him. He turned on his grandfather. 'You planted it for me to find . . . You sent me the note. It wasn't the Underground,' he said, his voice almost a whisper.

'I helped you make your mind up, that's all,' his grandfather said, a malevolent smile creeping across his face. 'You wanted to sign the Declaration and I took away the barriers, that's all. I was helping you.'

'Helping me?' Peter looked around the room wildly, adrenaline streaming through his veins so that he didn't know what to do with himself. 'You think that making me think I was infertile, having to tell Anna that she . . . that she . . .' He broke off, unable to finish the sentence, bending over involuntarily and crying out from the pain as the guards pulled his arms backwards.

'Take him away now,' Richard said, dismissing the guards with a wave. 'And Peter?' He looked at his grandson, his eyes narrowing. 'Make no mistake, if you do not follow my precise orders at the press conference, if you are not utterly convincing, Anna will be imprisoned for the rest of her life. You will never see her or her brother Ben again. And you yourself will be imprisoned for suspected aiding and abetting. Don't cross me, Peter. Trust me when I tell you that it really isn't worth it.'

Peter felt his fists clench with anger. 'Anna's Declaration,' he shouted as he was dragged from the room. 'Her signed Declaration. Was that you, too?'

But he got no answer.

'I thought you said the girl was dangerous?' Hillary whispered to Richard when the door had closed behind him and the guards. 'Are you really going to let her off the hook?'

Richard smiled darkly. 'Of course not,' he said. 'Far from it, in fact.'

Jude found himself at a dead end. He knew the lift shaft was only a few metres away, but a metal screen was blocking his way. He knocked it; it was thin, could be dismantled, he reckoned, but it would make a noise and the game would be up. Frustrated, he wriggled backwards; he would have to find another way round. Making his way back to the area above the Pincent Pharma reception, he crawled to the left. The dust was getting in his eyes and he longed to wipe it away, but each time he tried he simply added more; instead, he found himself squinting, using his hands to guide him.

And then, just when he thought he was making progress, he hit another dead end. Another metal plate – they must have been installed to separate the lift shaft, he realised. Whichever way round he went, he was going to find the same barrier. Sighing, he allowed himself to collapse on the floor in exhaustion whilst he collected his thoughts. He lay there for a few minutes, his mind racing, trying to work out what to do next. And then he heard something beneath him: a door opening. Tensing up, he lifted himself back on to his hands and knees; the guards had tracked him down, he realised. He'd been stupid to rest, even for a minute. But as he peeked down the nearest air vent to see how many guards there were, he frowned. One guard walked in, and didn't look up to the ceiling at all, but instead stared at the empty bench in front of him. His eyes scanned the room suspiciously, his hand reaching down to his holster to retrieve his gun. And then, suddenly, he fell to the ground. It took Jude a few seconds to realise that someone had struck him; his eyes widened as he realised that the someone was Pip, who had been hiding behind the door. Then he watched in disbelief as Pip swiftly unrobed the guard, swapped clothes with him and propped him up on the bench.

Chapter Twenty-seven

Pip cautiously opened the door and slipped into the corridor. Years of experience had taught him how to become invisible, to deflect attention, to blend seamlessly into the background, years that he seldom regretted and yet knew were owed to the darkest travails of humanity. The irony was not lost on him; in quiet moments he liked to muse on it, to question himself, just as he liked to question everything.

He took out his phone and dialled a number. 'Yes. Me. I'm in. There's a power cut here. Any information?'

'Power cut? No, no information. Your whereabouts?'

Pip frowned. The power cut couldn't be a happy accident; such things didn't exist. Was it Peter? A more malevolent force? He walked towards a small sign. 'Corridor A, North.'

'Roger. Contact will be with you shortly.'

Pip nodded. 'The power cut means security is compromised. Make your way in through the basement. But be careful – it might be a trap.'

'Roger.'

Unsettled, Pip turned his phone off and slipped out into the corridor. He disliked the things – he needed them, of course, knew they were invaluable, but even with anti-tracking devices they were dangerous. If he were caught, he would never give up his comrades, never alert the Authorities to the existence of a van full of men waiting to assist him when he gave the word. But his phone? It wouldn't take much to trace his last calls, to track down his fellow Underground soldiers.

Seconds later, a man in overalls appeared. He cleared his throat as he passed Pip, but kept on walking.

'Longevity's all very well, but a drug for tiredness would be welcome,' Pip said softly.

The man stopped. 'And one for heating,' he said hesitantly. 'I can't seem to warm up in this weather.'

They eyed each other for a couple of seconds, then Pip moved closer. 'Location?' he asked. 'Do we know where the girl is?' The news of Anna's kidnap – and it was a kidnap, as far as the Underground were concerned – had reached him just hours before from the watchers he'd assigned to shadow her. Immediately an action plan had been decided, contacts within Pincent Pharma rallied.

The man nodded and slipped a roughly drawn map into Pip's hand. 'She's being kept on the other side of the building, storeroom 48. But there's a guard outside.'

Pip nodded thoughtfully. 'What about the black-out?' he asked. 'What's the word?'

The man looked at him curiously. 'I thought that was you. They're saying it's the Underground.'

Pip frowned. 'Thank you,' he said sincerely. 'We'll be in touch.'

The man nodded briefly, then walked quickly away, back to work. He had risked his life and Pip knew that – cameras had probably picked up their exchange; within hours he might be questioned, tortured. But those hours would give Pip the time he needed. He had to think of the big picture. All of them did.

Adopting the gait of a guard, Pip walked off down the corridor. It took him several minutes to reach the services area where the storerooms were located on the other side of the building. His eyes scanned the numbers on the doors. He could hear the muffled sound of a baby crying, a sound which nearly stopped him in his tracks. Room 48 was just ahead; as his contact had warned him, a guard was stationed outside the room.

'Thought you might want a tea break,' he said to the guard.

The guard looked straight ahead. 'I'm not to move,' he said. 'Orders from Richard Pincent. Who are you, anyway? Don't remember seeing you around.'

Pip smiled. His hypnotic eyes looked steadily into the guard's, charming the look of suspicion from his face. 'Got brought down here to bolster security.

Because of the blackout,' he said. 'Just thought you might want to stretch your legs.'

The guard looked at him, a flicker of temptation crossing his eyes, then he shook his head. 'Not worth my while,' he said, raising his eyebrows. 'But cheers, all the same.'

'No problem. No problem at all.'

Pip smiled wryly, his eyes taking in every detail of the guard, of the door. Then he turned around and walked away. It was never going to be that easy, he thought to himself ruefully. But it had been worth a try.

The guards had to literally drag Peter through the warehouses, down the steps, down the corridor. At every stage he wrestled with them, cursed them, dragged his feet, protested.

'You know what they're doing up there?' he asked them, through gritted teeth. 'Do you know what Pincent Pharma does behind closed doors?' But the guards didn't seem interested; they stared resolutely ahead, kicking or pushing him every so often when he struggled too much, when irritation got the better of them. Eventually, Peter gave up; angrily, he looked down at the floor, the only place he could bear to look, the only place where he would not be met with posters proclaiming Longevity's wondrous properties, with whiteness, with the purity that permeated the entire building, purity that Peter now saw as the lure of the devil.

'Lifts are out,' one of the guards sighed. 'We'll have to take the stairs down.' They dragged Peter towards the stairwell, then pushed him down in front of them, chuckling when he stumbled, looking at him blankly when he turned to remonstrate with them.

As they reached the second floor, Peter heard footsteps beneath him, on their way up. A check over the banister revealed another guard, coming towards them. Could he trip him, Peter wondered? Could he create enough of a diversion to escape? Then he shook himself. Anna. He had to protect Anna. He had to do what his grandfather said. With a sigh, he continued to walk; seconds later, he came face to face with the approaching guard. The guard stopped; Peter stopped too, allowing his eyes to register the polished shoes, the dull grey uniform, the gold buttons. The eyes . . .

Peter felt his heart skip a beat as the familiar blue eyes registered surprise for an instant. He stared into them, feeling their questions, their reassurance, their acceptance, their warnings all at once, each message received perfectly by Peter.

'This the lad?' Pip asked.

'The lad?' The guards looked at him uncertainly.

'Peter Pincent,' Pip said, his voice a sneer. 'I'm to take him downstairs. Apparently there's more trouble upstairs and you're needed.'

'What sort of trouble? Mr Pincent told us to lock him in one of the storerooms behind reception,' one of the guards said.

Pip raised an eyebrow. 'All I know is that it's all kicked off. And Mr Pincent, he's not happy.'

The guards looked at each other apprehensively then pushed Peter towards Pip before turning and climbing the stairs again.

Roughly, Pip grabbed Peter; then turned and pushed him down the stairs, causing Peter to stumble. 'Get a move on,' he said tersely. 'I've got enough to do without babysitting, do you understand? Now come on, move.'

Peter started to walk, but Pip quickly stopped him, then put his finger to his lips and crept up after the guards. Peter heard two dull thuds and they both fell to the floor; Pip was holding what looked like a revolver, which he returned to his guard's holster. He bent over the guards, located their keys and in a few seconds had released Peter's handcuffs.

'Quick, help me move them,' he whispered. They dragged the bodies down to the second floor landing, and Peter acted as a lookout while Pip found an empty room to stash them in.

'Right. To the storerooms,' Pip said when he'd finished. 'After you.'

He held the door to the stairwell open for Peter, who walked through it, his legs feeling unsteady.

'You . . . you know where they are?' Peter managed to say.

'I have a feeling I might,' Pip said, taking the map from his pocket. He pulled Peter down the stairs then motioned towards a door, leading to a long, empty corridor. Peter followed, silently; moments later, Pip opened a door leading to an empty room.

'Quick,' he said. 'We haven't got long. What's going on? Did you cause the blackout? Why the guards?'

Peter felt his heart thumping. 'Anna,' he said, ignoring Pip's questions. 'My grandfather . . . he said she's been arrested. He said she'd been caught planning seditious activities.'

'She was trapped,' Pip said calmly. 'That's why we came here – to get her out.'

'She's here? I thought she was in prison somewhere. Who's the "we" anyway? Are you here with other people?'

Pip nodded.

'Then tell them we need them to storm this place,' Peter said, his voice rising with emotion. 'To get Anna out, but also . . .' he paused, his eyes widening as he looked at Pip. 'They have to go to Unit X. I was there. That's why my grandfather . . . the guards, I mean. It was because I saw what he's doing up there. He had Sheila, and other Surplus girls. They were . . . They're harvesting foetuses, Pip. For Longevity+. I had to leave her there. I have to sign the Declaration, otherwise Anna . . .' His voice dried up as he felt his legs buckling beneath him and he slowly slid to the ground. 'I didn't listen to you,' he whispered. 'I didn't listen . . .'

'You discovered the truth,' Pip said, seeming to take this torrent of information in his stride. 'Better to find your own way than to blindly trust the words of others, whoever they are.' He leant down and put his hand on Peter's shoulder. 'But now you know the truth, we must get you both out of here.'

'I didn't protect Anna,' Peter said desperately. 'I said I would, and I failed her. I told her to sign. I . . .' He gulped, forcing back the tears that had welled up in his eyes. 'And it was all a lie. The sterilisation programme. He made it all up.'

'A lie?' Pip's face lit up. 'Yes, yes, I hoped . . .'

'I hate myself,' Peter whispered.

'You should despise Richard Pincent, but not yourself,' Pip said gently. 'Richard Pincent is determined to twist the world to his own dark ends; you are on the side of the angels. But even angels fall, sometimes. We all make mistakes; without them we would learn nothing.'

'You don't make mistakes,' Peter said despondently.

Pip turned away. 'I have made the worst mistakes of all,' he said quietly. 'But we can all strive to make amends. That is why I fight, Peter. That is why I continue to take Longevity, the drug I despise, why I keep myself alive – because I won't stop until it's over. Until it's all over.'

Peter looked at him searchingly. His mentor, the man he had once considered invincible, all-knowing, all-seeing, suddenly seemed frail, human.

'So what are we waiting for?' he said. 'Let's get them out. Let's attack.'

Pip shook his head. 'No, Peter. We can't risk it.'

'But why?' Peter said desperately. 'We need to get

the girls out. You didn't see it, Pip, it was horrible.'

'I know,' Pip said seriously. 'But an armed attack would bring the security forces down on us. No, we need to do this quietly.'

'Quietly,' Peter sighed with frustration. Then he frowned. 'So who caused the blackout? If it wasn't you, I mean?'

'I don't know,' Pip said, shaking his head. 'In former times I'd have said that God was on our side.'

'God?' Peter's eyebrows shot up. 'I thought he'd been replaced by my grandfather.'

As he spoke, there was a noise from above and they both looked up sharply. Then, seconds later, there was another noise, something scraping along the ceiling. Pip put his fingers to his lips and silently moved a chair under the air vent in the ceiling. Then he stood on it, lifted his hands up and quietly levered the air vent open.

Peter looked up apprehensively; the next thing he knew, Pip was dragging someone down through the vent on to the floor. Peter stepped back, his eyes wide, his heart racing in his chest and stared at the person on the ground. He didn't look like a Pincent Pharma employee; he was wearing jeans, his hair was too long, his face was . . . Peter frowned as he peered at him from the corner of the room. His face looked young. As young as Peter's own face.

Peter looked around for a makeshift weapon and grabbed a wooden pole, which closer inspection revealed to be a broom handle. He brandished it, held it over the youth as Pip knelt on top of him. But instead of flinching, he looked directly at Peter, and his expression wasn't one of fear, of fascination, or any of the usual emotions people displayed when seeing him for the first time; it was an expression Peter couldn't read – of sadness, perhaps, or loss.

'You know, it isn't God that's on your side,' the young man said, his voice strangled from Pip pressing down on his chest. 'To my knowledge, no god can leave a connectivity demon, untraceable by even the most experienced technological professional, particularly the lazy, ignorant computer geeks that work here. A connectivity demon that shuts down electricity across the whole building.'

Pip was peering at him. 'You!' he exclaimed, his voice full of surprise.

'Yeah, me,' the young man said. His face was dirty; his eyes alert.

'Who are you?' Peter demanded. 'What are you doing here?'

The young man stared at him. 'I'm here to get that girl out. The one with the red hair.'

'But who are you?' Peter was staring at him, his mouth wide open.

Jude bit his lip. 'I'm Jude . . .' he said, clearing his throat. 'I'm your half-brother.'

Chapter Twenty-eight

It took a few seconds for Peter to digest what Jude had said, then, bewildered, he could do nothing but stare uncomprehendingly at the dirty, dishevelled young man sitting on the floor.

'Half-brother?' he said eventually, staring at Jude in disbelief. 'Then you're . . .'

'Stephen Fitz-Patrick's son,' Jude choked. 'Jude 2124 at your service.' He tried to throw his shoulders back but his chest hurt and his throat had seized up. He'd rehearsed this speech, this meeting, so many times in his head – now he couldn't say anything, all he felt was pain.

'What are you doing here, Jude? I thought I told you to watch yourself?'

Jude stared at Pip in disbelief. 'What?' he asked incredulously. 'I'm helping, in case you didn't notice. You should have accepted my help before, too, when I offered.'

Pip shook his head, his expression serious. 'It was for your own good. And us. You know you're under surveillance by the Authorities?'

'Jude 2124?' Peter's face was still blank with incomprehension, confusion.

'My cipher,' Jude said, standing up and dusting himself down. 'And I can handle Authority surveillance, thank you very much. Guards here thought they could lock me up. Look how that turned out.' He shot Pip a triumphant glance.

'And you know Pip . . . ?' Peter asked.

'Yeah,' Jude said, coughing violently. 'We've met.'

'And you never told me?' Peter swung round to Pip.

'I didn't want to confuse you,' Pip said quietly. 'Not when there was already so much at stake.'

Peter turned back to Jude. 'You're really my brother? You're the one who . . .' He stepped forward, his eyes wide. He reached out tentatively as if to touch Jude, but he pulled back.

'Yeah,' Jude said. 'I'm the one who . . .' He shrugged. 'You know . . . who ruined your life.' He threw a defensive look at Pip.

Pip looked at him curiously. 'So it was you who caused the blackout? How did you even get in here?'

'I told you. The red-haired girl. She's in Unit X. I came to rescue her.'

'You know about Unit X?' Pip's eyes were flickering, as though calculating some difficult equation in his head.

'Yes, I know,' Jude said. 'I saw those guards grabbing Peter. I watched you on the security cameras . . .'

'How?' Peter demanded. 'The cameras aren't

working. Nothing's working.'

Jude allowed a small smile to creep on to his lips. 'Sure nothing's working. But when you're the person who stopped things working, you tend to know ways to get them working again.'

'I don't understand.'

Jude rolled his eyes. 'Mainframe's in the ceiling. Put it on emergency mode and you can still operate the cameras, only one by one. It's a default security measure.'

'Can you get it working again?' Pip asked immediately.

Jude nodded, casually. 'Don't need to, though. It'll come on by itself in a while.' He turned back to Peter, his eyes earnest. 'I'm sorry,' he said quietly. 'I'm really sorry. For everything. I'm the reason you were a Surplus.'

'Don't be stupid, it wasn't your fault. Why didn't you contact me before?'

'I couldn't. I didn't know what to say. I was afraid you'd . . . I was afraid.'

'Yeah? Thing is, I've always wanted a brother,' Peter said quietly.

Jude grinned. 'Me too. This is so cool.'

They stood silently, for a few seconds, then Peter turned to Pip. His mind was racing but he knew he had to focus. 'Anna,' he said. 'We have to save Anna. Now.'

'And the other girl,' Jude said firmly. 'We have to get her too.'

'We?' Pip turned to Jude. 'There is no we. This is a job for the Underground, not an amateur.' He looked at Peter. 'We'll get Anna. Then you must get out of here. Both of you. I and my men will deal with the girls.'

'I'm not going anywhere.' Jude folded his arms. 'Not until that girl's safe.'

'Me neither,' Peter said firmly. 'I'm going to get Anna out and then I'm going to speak at this press conference.'

'You can't stay for the press conference,' Pip said, his eyes staring directly into Peter's. 'You have to get out. We have to get you to safety – it's too dangerous here.'

Peter shook his head. 'It's too dangerous not to be here,' he said quietly. 'I have to stand up to him. I have to stop him . . .'

'But –'

'But nothing, Pip. I'm going to do this, whether you like it or not.'

'Me too,' Jude said firmly.

'See, Pip, there *is* a we.' Peter held out his hand; Jude shook it firmly.

Pip shook his head in defeat. 'Very well,' he said softly. 'But you do exactly as I say. No heroics, understand?'

'Loud and clear,' Peter said gratefully. 'And I'm sorry, Pip. About the other night. I'm sorry I didn't listen, sorry I didn't believe you.'

'Sorry?' Pip smiled. 'You don't need my forgiveness.

I'm simply a relic from the past who will soon outlive his usefulness, who can be too cautious, too untrusting, who closes doors which . . .' he looked over at Jude . . . 'which perhaps should have been kept open. Although I reserve judgement on that.'

'You're not a relic,' Peter said, allowing himself to grin in spite of the tension. 'Not quite yet.'

Chapter Twenty-nine

Dr Edwards looked up at the door hopefully.

'Peter?' he called. 'Come in. There's no need to knock.'

Peter appeared through the doorway; next to him, a guard stared at him intently.

Dr Edwards' forehead crumpled into a frown. 'Peter? Is everything OK?' He looked at the guard. 'Did you get lost on the way back here?'

Peter stepped forward. 'Dr Edwards, I need your help. We do, I mean.'

'Help?' Dr Edwards said curiously. 'Of course. What can I do?'

Peter cleared his throat. 'I . . . Anna's in trouble. She's here. And . . .'

'Here?'

'She's locked up.' Peter's face was pale. His fists were clenched and the muscles around his neck were tense. Dr Edwards frowned at the guard.

'Would you leave us?' he asked.

The guard shook his head.

'I see.' Dr Edwards stood up, took a deep breath

and looked back at Peter. 'I'm afraid I don't understand. Why on earth would Anna be here?'

'It was my grandfather,' Peter said, looking at him intently. 'He tricked her. He sent Catchers after her . . .'

'Catchers? But she's Legal. Peter, please sit down. I'm sure there's a perfectly good explanation –'

'Was there a perfectly good explanation last time you challenged Richard Pincent?' the guard asked suddenly.

Dr Edwards turned. 'I'm sorry? Are you talking to me?'

The guard nodded. 'You know as well as I do that Richard Pincent is a dangerous man. And you know as well as I do that there are things going on within these walls. Things which Richard Pincent would do anything to protect from prying eyes. Even if it means imprisoning Anna. Blackmailing Peter.'

'Blackmail?' Dr Edwards' eyes widened. 'Who are you?' he asked the guard. 'Who is this man?' he asked Peter.

Peter stepped forward. 'He's . . . a friend,' he said tentatively. 'He's come to help me.'

'A friend?' Dr Edwards faltered slightly. 'He's . . . He's not a guard, is he?' he said, his voice a whisper now.

Peter shook his head.

The man turned his gaze to Dr Edwards. He had the most incredible blue eyes. Dr Edwards thought he remembered eyes like that from somewhere, but it was impossible. Those eyes . . . they were from another time.

'You questioned Richard Pincent's methods and you were sidelined because you didn't like what he was doing. Now Peter thinks you'll help us. To be honest, I'm not sure you're up to it, but we don't have many options here, so what's it going to be?'

'It *is* you,' Dr Edwards said suddenly. 'It's . . .'

'Pip, I go by Pip now. We studied together, you see, Peter,' Pip said levelly, still holding Dr Edwards' gaze. 'Many years ago. Dr Edwards was always top of the class. Cleverest scientist of his generation. And since there weren't many more generations, that makes him one of the cleverest men alive.' The way he said it didn't sound like a compliment.

'You were a scientist?' Peter looked at Pip incredulously.

'I used to be,' Pip said flatly. 'And now,' he said, addressing Dr Edwards, 'now you're working at Pincent Pharma. Only you're not really, are you? I mean, ReTraining. It's hardly a prestigious post, is it?'

Dr Edwards blanched slightly. 'Training is important. Imparting knowledge . . .'

'To who? There's no one to teach,' Pip said. 'Not any more. You've been pushed out of research into semi-retirement. Isn't that closer to the truth?'

'I chose to leave,' Dr Edwards said firmly. 'No one was pushed out of anything.' He faltered slightly, reached out to his desk to steady himself.

'And now you're fully involved in the development

of Longevity+? You know what it is they're doing?' Pip's eyes were boring into Dr Edwards' and he felt beads of sweat begin to form on his forehead.

'No . . . I mean . . . it's highly secret.' Dr Edwards thought uncomfortably of his visit to the lab technicians that afternoon – a visit in which his former colleagues had been evasive, even secretive. A few years ago, he'd have challenged them, tried to discover the truth; now he barely even noticed, had lost the will to even care.

'So secret that you, an eminent scientist, are being kept out? So secret that you haven't even been invited to the press conference this afternoon?'

'Press conference? No, that's not my field. That's not . . .' He cleared his throat, forced his shoulders back. 'I don't expect to be kept informed of press conferences. I train people, I train the scientists of the future. I prefer it that way.'

'The scientists of the future or the accountants of the past who are bored of their old jobs and looking for something to fill their time for a few years?' Pip asked. His voice was softer now and more compelling for it.

Dr Edwards' shoulders sagged slightly. 'ReTraining is a good initiative,' he said weakly. 'It enables people to reinvent themselves, to reinvigorate their careers.'

'He's a great teacher,' Peter said suddenly. 'Pip, leave him alone. It isn't Dr Edwards' fault about Anna or the other Surpluses. He didn't know.'

'Other Surpluses?' Dr Edwards asked. He felt his

chest constricting.

'You remember,' Pip said levelly. 'That was what you disagreed with Richard Pincent about, wasn't it? The use of Surpluses?'

'He said they wouldn't . . . He said . . .' Dr Edwards said weakly.

'I'm sure he did,' Pip said. 'I'm sure he said a lot of things.'

Dr Edwards frowned uncomfortably and turned to Peter. 'You say Anna's in danger? What sort of danger?'

'He says she's going to prison. If I don't sign the Declaration, I mean. He's got her locked up. Dr Edwards, please, we need your help.'

'My help? But what can I do?'

'You can stand up for what you believe in,' Pip said gravely. 'Help Peter to save Anna. Attend the press conference and tell the journalists anything you know. I have men downstairs who can help you, who can get you to safety afterwards.'

Dr Edwards could feel his legs trembling beneath him ominously. He hadn't spoken out for a long time. A very long time. Then he nodded. It had been too long, he realised. It was time to make amends. 'Very well,' he said quietly, picking up his lab coat. 'If I can help to stop this . . . Then yes, of course.'

Chapter Thirty

'How are we going to do this?' Peter asked anxiously. 'Even if we can get Anna out of her cell and the Surpluses out of Unit X, how will we get them away from the building?'

'There's a back entrance, where the lorries come in. It'll be manned, but we've got men in the basement waiting for my signal,' Pip said calmly. 'And as for the Pincent guards, they'll be concentrating on the front of the building. There's a press conference in an hour or so, remember. You and Peter focus on getting Anna to the back entrance; I'll arrange to have my men meet you with transport.'

'Transport? Here? How? Nothing will get through,' Dr Edwards said. 'All the roads will be blocked.'

Pip smiled wryly. 'Nothing? Oh, I doubt that. I imagine that Anna might enjoy a jaunt on the river. What do you think?'

Peter felt the familiar reassurance and gratitude that the Underground existed, that they were on his side. He'd missed that feeling; felt guilty for having doubted Pip.

'What about the Surpluses?' he asked.

'Leave them to me,' Pip said firmly. 'Jude and I will look after them.'

'Good luck,' Dr Edwards said. His eyes met Pip's for a second or two, a bond of trust passing between them, a pact, and then they both turned to Peter.

'Ready?' Pip whispered.

'Ready,' Peter whispered back, as Dr Edwards opened the door.

Dr Edwards had never been to the services corridor at the back of the building – the rooms were largely store cupboards, workrooms, areas where men in overalls usually roamed with large hands covered in dirt and grease. He looked over at Peter, who met his eye and nodded tightly, before dropping back. Dr Edwards continued down the corridor, barely daring to look anywhere but straight ahead. And then he stopped. The light was dim but Dr Edwards could see the guard Pip had told them about, sitting outside Room 48, his expression one of intense boredom.

A mild feeling of discomfort made Dr Edwards slow down slightly. He hated confrontation, hated challenges unless they were written down in academic papers and read out at seminars. Perhaps Pip and Peter were wrong, he found himself hoping. Perhaps there was a perfectly reasonable explanation after all.

Taking a deep breath, he approached the door and smiled at the guard. 'May I?' he asked, holding his hand towards the lock.

The guard shook his head. 'Only Mr Pincent and the doctor's allowed in there,' he said firmly.

The feeling of discomfort became more intense, and Dr Edwards stepped back. 'But I am a doctor,' he said. 'I'm Dr Edwards.'

'Only Dr Ferguson's allowed in,' the guard said flatly. 'And he's been in already.'

'Dr Ferguson?' Dr Edwards managed to keep the smile on his face at the mention of a man he despised. A man he'd been under the impression had left Pincent Pharma years ago, never to return. 'So, he's back, is he?'

'Never went away, so far as I know.'

'Indeed.' Dr Edwards took out his identi-card. 'Well, you should also know that I am Head of ReTraining at Pincent Pharma, and that I am here to see the girl on a matter of high importance.'

The guard looked at his card. 'No one said anything about ReTraining. I'm afraid you can't go in.'

Dr Edwards caught the guard's eye and nodded curtly. 'Then I shall have to call Mr Pincent. Even though he has asked not to be disturbed. Can you tell me your guard number please?'

'Four-three-one,' he said. 'And you call him. I know my orders.'

'Four-three-one,' Dr Edwards said, his heart pounding in his chest, every hair on his body standing erect. He took out his phone, pretended to call Richard.

'Yes?' said Pip at the other end.

'Mr Pincent. I wish to see the prisoner. Would you

mind sending order to the guard please?'

'You're stalling,' Pip replied. 'You've got the stun gun. Use it.'

'Thank you,' Dr Edwards said. 'I'll wait here.'

The guard looked up. 'I'm going to get the order, am I?' he asked.

'Any minute now,' Dr Edwards said. His hands were trembling as he took out the gun. The guard was looking expectantly at his walkie-talkie; he didn't even have time to look up before the sedative took effect.

'Peter,' Dr Edwards hissed, but Peter was already beside him, having watched the whole thing.

'Get his key.'

Dr Edwards moved towards the guard tentatively, pulling him on to his side. And then something made him retch. There was blood. On his jacket.

'It's a stun gun,' he said, his voice a whisper. 'Pip said it was a stun gun. Why is he bleeding? Why would he . . .' He felt the guard's pulse – nothing.

Immediately Dr Edwards fell to his knees. 'I killed him! I killed a man.' His hands were in his hair, his brain racing with shock, with incomprehension.

'You killed a guard,' Peter corrected him. 'And there's no time for this. Come on, we have to get to Anna.'

Peter pulled the keys from the guard's belt loop and opened the door then heaved the body through it; Dr Edwards, still in a state of shock, helped him. The room was dark except for emergency lighting which bathed the floor with a warm glow; he could make out the figure of a girl, sitting on a hard chair, her expression anxious; the only sound in the room was the rasping breathing of the baby she was clutching to her. She looked at his white lab coat, the Pincent Pharma photo ID pinned to his chest pocket and shrank back.

'Anna!' Peter rushed over to her. 'What happened?'

'Peter?' Anna jumped up, her expression changing from fear to amazement, and hurled her arms round his neck. 'Oh, Peter, I'm so sorry. I didn't mean to let you down . . .'

'You could never let me down,' Peter said tightly. 'Never.' He took her in his arms, and she flinched a little. Then he frowned. 'You're hurt,' he said angrily. 'What have they done to you?'

'Nothing,' Anna said quickly. 'Just the guards, they . . . It's nothing, really. But there was a doctor. He said he needed to do some . . . investigations,' she said, looking at Dr Edwards. 'But it's Ben who needs a doctor. I think he's ill. I think he needs help.'

Dr Edwards moved towards Anna and felt the baby's head; it was burning up.

'Why are you here?' he asked, relieved to have another focus. 'Who brought you?'

Anna looked up at him, wide-eyed. 'The police. The Catchers. He said Maria was a Catcher. I thought Maria wanted to save the children and I wanted to help . . . I wanted to . . .' As she spoke, fat tears began to cascade down her cheeks. 'I'm sorry,' she choked.

'I'm sorry . . .'

'Don't be sorry,' Peter pulled her into him gently. 'Don't ever be sorry, Anna. This is all my fault . . .'

Dr Edwards looked around the room. On a small table in the corner sat a file; quickly he picked it up and crouching low, close to the light, he started to read. Then he swung round.

'These medical investigations,' he said, his voice catching as he spoke. 'Do you know what they were for?'

Anna shook her head and Dr Edwards felt his shoulders tighten with determination, with anger – at Richard for what he'd done, at himself for not knowing about it.

'Anna,' Peter whispered, 'we're going to get you out of here. We're going to get you a long way away. Pip's here. And the Underground. They're waiting for you. Waiting to help.'

'Pip? He's here?'

Peter nodded. 'There are Surpluses here,' he whispered tightly. 'I followed my grandfather. I found Unit X.'

'Unit X?'

'They've got Surpluses there. They're pregnant. He's using them for Longevity+. Embryonic stem cells. They're . . .' He looked away, the image of Sheila making him shudder involuntarily.

'They're not the only ones,' Dr Edwards said, his voice strained.

'Not the only ones what?'

Dr Edwards met Peter's eye then looked at Anna. 'I mean they're not the only ones who are pregnant.'

'You mean there are more?' Peter said bitterly.

'Not the Surpluses,' Dr Edwards whispered. 'Anna. Your notes,' he said, turning to Anna. 'You're pregnant, Anna. And according to this file, they want to . . . They . . .' Dr Edwards couldn't bring himself to repeat what he'd read, the abbreviations he knew all too well, abbreviations that he'd pushed from his mind for years.

Peter looked at Dr Edwards uncertainly. 'She's pregnant? Anna's pregnant?'

'But the Surplus Sterilisation programme,' Anna said, her voice several octaves higher than usual. 'I can't be. I . . .'

'It didn't exist,' Peter said, grabbing her and holding her tight. 'It never got ratified. My grandfather . . . he left that file for me on purpose. He sent me a note, one that looked like it was from the Underground, just so that I'd find it, the programme file. But it was never passed. He just wanted me to sign, that's all.'

'So I'm pregnant? I'm really pregnant?' Anna gasped.

'Yes, Anna. You're going to have a baby.'

A huge smile filled Anna's pale face, brought to life her worried eyes. Peter suddenly pulled away and stared at her in disbelief, in horror.

'And I was going to . . . I got you to . . .' Frantically, he reached into his back pocket and took out a large piece of paper, ripping it up into as many pieces as he could, before throwing them on the ground. 'Your Declaration,' he said, taking Anna in his arms again and burying his head in her neck. 'You signed it because of me. And I'll never forgive myself. But it's gone now.' He kissed her. 'I've been so stupid. So completely stupid.'

'Not stupid,' Dr Edward said quietly, looking at the guard's slumped body. 'Sometimes we trust when we shouldn't. Your grandfather is a very wicked man, Peter. He needs to be stopped. Whatever it takes.'

'I'm going to do more than that,' Peter said fiercely. 'I'm going to destroy him.'

Chapter Thirty-one

Following Peter's directions, Pip edged along the side of the wall of the great warehouse-like rooms, stealthily, silently. His guard's uniform had enabled him to pass easily through the building and up the stairs to the sixth floor; he knew that from his vantage point above the Security Centre, Jude would be watching his progress silently as he flicked from camera to camera.

There were voices, suddenly, and Pip hung back in the shadows as two men passed, talking in low voices.

'It doesn't matter anyway. From tomorrow, this will all be official.'

'You trust that Authorities woman?'

'It's not a matter of trust. She can't afford not to approve us. The revenue generation will be huge. Jobs, energy, everyone's wellbeing – it's a no-brainer. Stop worrying.'

'I'm not worrying.'

They didn't see Pip; they walked straight past him, out of the door and down the stairs. Carefully, Pip inched forwards towards the door from which they'd emerged, trusting, hoping that Jude was in place, that he was watching, that he was ready. Then, tentatively, he opened it just a fraction, immediately blinking against the bright lights. There were two nurses in the room, sitting in the corner at a table, chatting. Otherwise the room was in silence. Next to the door was an intercom phone and two light switches; silently, Pip looked up at the camera, nodded. His trust in Jude was rewarded seconds later when the lights suddenly went out, and Pip slipped through the door.

Immediately he heard the sound of footsteps rushing over.

'The blackout's spreading,' a nurse said anxiously.

'Hello? Hello? Oh, for God's sake, the intercom's gone dead.'

'What do we do?'

'We'd better let them know downstairs.'

Pip moved quickly in the dark and grabbed the nurse nearest the door. She screamed. 'Up against the wall,' he barked.

'What? Who's there? Who said that?'

'I've got a gun. I want you up against the wall, all of you.'

He heard yelps and scrambling, then took out a torch, shining it around the room, assuring himself that no one was hiding from him. 'Turn around,' he ordered. 'Arms above your heads.'

'But the guards . . . The guards will be here in minutes. Are you mad? You can't just walk in here and . . .'

'I can do what I like,' he said, through gritted teeth.

Pip picked up a towel and ordered a nurse to gag the doctor who was speaking, then to tie up the others; finally, he tied her up. Then, quickly, he ran to the beds. 'Sheila?' he asked, looking from girl to girl, his heart aching at what he saw.

A girl looked up sleepily. 'Was I Valuable?' she asked dozily. 'Can I go back to Grange Hall now?'

'Not to Grange Hall,' Pip said, his voice tightening as he rushed over to her. 'But let's see if we can't get you somewhere safe, OK? Let's see if we can't get all of you out of here.'

He took out his phone and made a call to the men waiting in the basement of the building. 'I'm in,' he said simply. 'I'm going to need four men up here now.'

'Samuels?'

Derek Samuels moved his receiver to his ear immediately. 'Yes? Mr Pincent?'

'The press conference will be starting at six o'clock sharp. I need you to collect Peter.'

'Of course. I'll be there right away.'

'Good.'

Derek Samuels wiped a trickle of sweat off his forehead as he looked down at Guard 431, who was slumped against the wall beside the cell door, the girl gone. Another guard had been found dead in the waiting room off reception. Two more in a room off the second-floor landing. Taking his gun out and holding it close to his chest, he called a guard to move the body.

'Where've you been?' Dr Edwards whispered anxiously. 'The guards will be on to us any second now.'

They were in the basement as arranged; Pip, whose face had just appeared around the corner, grimaced. 'You got Anna?' he asked.

'Yes. She's here with me.'

Pip saw her thin frame standing behind Dr Edwards, and he nodded, then disappeared. Seconds later, he emerged again, a girl draped over his arms. Behind him four men were also carrying young girls. Underground men, Dr Edwards realised. Underground soldiers. 'Good, because we need your help to get these girls out, now.'

Dr Edwards' eyes widened. 'Of course,' he said. 'They're from Unit X?'

Pip nodded. 'Where's Peter?'

'Back in his cell.'

'Good. The boat's waiting. Take Sheila.'

He handed the girl in his arms to Dr Edwards, who took her gingerly.

'Sheila? Is that really you?' It was Anna talking; Sheila didn't answer, but Anna took her hand nevertheless, squeezed it, planted herself beside her like a guard. She was so fragile, Dr Edwards thought to himself as he looked down at Sheila's small frame and red hair, but her lightness only compounded the weight that he had felt bearing down on him since

Peter and Pip had come into his laboratory that afternoon, since he'd discovered the truth about what was happening within these walls. He was complicit, he'd realised; he hadn't done enough to stop it, had allowed Richard Pincent to bully him, to silence him. And these girls had paid the price. Slowly, heavily, he turned around and started walking back down the stairs, Anna beside him. Pip went ahead to secure their path; a few feet behind him, the four Underground soldiers followed. Stealthily, they made their way out of the basement to the loading bay where the rest of the Underground men were waiting in the winter darkness. Silently, he followed Pip, turning right out of the exit and following the wall of the building until they reached the marshland leading to the river. Their feet squelching in the boggy grass, they began to walk more quickly until finally they reached the boat, a sizeable armoured speedboat nestling against the river's edge.

'The tide's low so you'll have to jump,' Pip said to Anna. 'We'll pass Ben down to you.'

Nodding bravely, Anna took a deep breath and jumped over the edge of the river bank, landing safely on the boat, then she reached up her hands for her brother.

The girls, groggy and sleepy, were passed down next; they half fell on to the boat where Anna quickly sat them up, pulling their gowns down where they had risen up, exposing the girls, leeching yet more dignity from them. Finally, the Underground soldiers themselves followed, hauling themselves down the bank and on to the boat below.

'You should go with them,' Pip said to Dr Edwards.

Dr Edwards looked at the boat, then shook his head. 'No,' he said. 'You wanted me at the press conference.'

'That was before you killed a guard and helped a prisoner and the Surpluses to escape. You won't make it to the press conference. Go now. We'll keep you hidden.'

Dr Edwards looked at the girls, at Anna, then back at Pip. 'You know, this place has been my life,' he said, his voice quiet. 'Science has been my life for as long as I can remember. I thought I was seeking truth. I thought science was beautiful.'

'Science can be beautiful,' Pip said. 'But good science, not bad.'

'One can turn into the other so easily. I saw Longevity as the saviour of mankind. How can something so healing be so destructive?'

'All beauty has a dark side. Heaven can't exist without hell.'

Dr Edwards grimaced. 'To discover, though, that you are on the side of the devils . . .' he whispered. He looked back at Pincent Pharma with disgust.

'It's not your fault,' Pip said, carefully, then he forced a smile. 'Anyway, there's always an Authorities ReTraining programme. What do they say? "Long Lives, New Challenges"?'

Dr Edwards caught his eye. 'ReTraining,' he said

quietly. 'Yes, of course. The truth is . . .'

'Stop right there.' Dr Edwards heard a voice shouting from behind them and turned around to be greeted by a flashlight and a uniformed figure approaching through the darkness. He immediately saw the glint of a gun in the guard's hand.

'Guard,' he called out. 'I can explain.'

'No explanation required,' the guard said. 'Move an inch and you're dead, both of you.' He took out his walkie-talkie. 'Back-up requested, back entrance, river frontage.'

'Of course,' Dr Edwards said, his mind working frantically. In moments, more guards would appear, he, Pip and the girls would be captured.

'Guard, there's no need for this,' he said, then, affecting what he hoped was a confident, reassuring tone. 'I thought I heard something, that's all. Came out to investigate.' Then he turned to Pip. 'Go,' he hissed, as the guard's location was confirmed by a tinny-sounding voice. 'Get out of here.'

'I'm not leaving you here,' Pip said, under his breath. 'There's no need. We can take this guard.'

'There'll be more in minutes,' Dr Edwards whispered back. 'It's not worth the risk.'

'But he'll kill you,' Pip said. 'You know he will.'

The guard, who had halted some metres away, was staring at them impassively, pointing his gun at one of them, then the other, then back again. Not far away, Dr Edwards could hear the thud of boots on hard ground, the sound of running.

'You know, death isn't as scary as I thought it would be,' he said, his voice soft, but loud enough for Pip to hear. 'Perhaps Peter was right about it being nature's version of Renewal after all.' He turned back, briefly, and smiled. 'Tell him he was right. Tell him forever isn't important – it's now that counts. Doing the right thing. Finally . . .'

Giving Pip one last look, he started to walk towards the guard, his hands up in the air. 'Really, Guard, there's no reason to be like this. If you'd just let me explain . . .'

'Explain? I don't want an explanation. Stay where you are or I'll shoot.' The guard was squinting at him; Dr Edwards had positioned himself in the glare of his flashlight.

'But we're on the same side,' Dr Edwards continued, watching as Pip shot him one last look before ducking down over the river bank out of sight.

'Stop moving immediately or I'll shoot,' the guard said, angry now. 'Come one more step . . .'

'One more? You'd shoot me just for one more step?' Dr Edwards asked, continuing to walk. But his words were drowned out by the sound of a pistol firing; as he landed on the mud, he felt the blissful sensation of pain shooting around his body, cleansing his sins, freeing him from anguish. He heard the guard erupt in anger as he realised that Pip had disappeared, heard him barking at the other guards arriving on the scene to search along the river's edge. But as his life ebbed away, Dr Edwards heard the unmistakable sound of a boat's engine starting up, and as he closed his eyes, he knew the guards were already too late.

Chapter Thirty-two

Derek Samuels watched over the shoulder of the programmer, suppressing the desire to shoot him in the head for failing miserably to restore power. He was not a man who ever allowed himself to lose control, but today he was close. 'The press conference is due to start in fifteen minutes,' he said, his voice low and menacing, 'and if energy is not restored, if Mr Pincent is forced to cancel, then you and your family will live to regret it.'

The programmer, who was sweating profusely, nodded. He'd had his entire team scanning every interface, every programme, every connection, and still he'd found nothing. 'We're doing everything we can,' he said, his voice tight with stress. 'We can't find the problem, that's the thing. Everything's as it should be.'

'Everything is evidently not as it should be, otherwise it would be working,' Mr Samuels snarled. 'I don't have time for this. Get this thing working now.'

The programmer was sweating. 'Yes, sir,' he said, wiping his forehead with his sleeve. 'Yes, sir, I'll just

. . .' He was interrupted by a flash of light, a sound of whirring, of machines coming back to life. He had no idea why – it wasn't anything he'd done – but it was the most beautiful sound he had ever heard. He stared at his screen for a few moments, not daring to believe energy was restored, then, slowly, a smile crept its way across his face. 'There we are,' he said tentatively. 'I think you'll find it's fixed.'

Derek Samuels opened the door, saw that the lights were indeed on along the corridor, that the electronic locks were once again working. 'What did you do?' he demanded. 'What was the problem? Was it sabotage? Was it interference or a system failure?'

The programmer smiled uncertainly. 'It was . . . a system failure,' he said, after a brief pause in which he'd worked out that a terrorist attack would require him to point out what the attackers did, something that he knew he was unable to do.

'I see,' Samuels said darkly. 'And it took you this long to work out the problem?'

'I've only been here an hour,' the programmer pointed out, his confidence returning. 'And it's fixed, isn't it?'

'For all I know, you could have caused the problem in the first place. For all I know, you could be an Underground supporter.'

'An Underground supporter?' The programmer's eyes widened. 'Why would I support them? I'm just doing my job. I'm just . . .'

'Never mind,' Samuels said curtly. 'You'll stay here

until we know exactly what happened.' He looked over to the guard. 'Bring the Fitz-Patrick boy here.'

Minutes later, Jude appeared, pushed into the room by the guard. His clothes were stained and torn, his face streaked with black dust.

Derek Samuels looked him up and down. 'You've been busy,' he said evenly.

'I've been trying to get out,' Jude said sullenly. 'You left me in a cupboard and I'm claustrophobic. The lights went out. I didn't know what to do.'

'You were trying to get out? Of Pincent Pharma? That's interesting. I heard that someone has been clambering about above our ceilings. That wouldn't be you, I suppose?'

Jude raised an eyebrow. 'Not that I know of,' he said, shrugging. 'Anyway, I didn't manage to get out, did I? So can I go now?'

'Go?' Mr Samuels smiled thinly. 'Oh, I don't think you are going anywhere, Jude. You see, we take breaches of our security very seriously, as do the Authorities. We take the lives of our guards very seriously. We take attacks on our energy supply very seriously, too. So I want you to sit down here and have a little think, because if you know anything about what's happened here today, you are going to tell me, do you understand? Guard, take the programmer away and . . . look after him, will you?'

The guard nodded, immediately, and pulled the programmer from his chair, who shot a terrified look in Jude's direction before stumbling out of the room.

Richard Pincent slammed down the phone and looked over at Hillary who was sitting primly on a sofa near his desk.

'You see?' he said, relief surging through him and a look of triumph spread all over his face. 'Energy has been restored.'

'And the culprit?'

'Information will be passed to the Authorities at the relevant time,' Richard said. 'Investigations are still underway.'

'Good. Because we will want to see a comprehensive report. Security breaches at Pincent Pharma reflect badly on the Authorities, Richard. They raise all sorts of questions about competence. And there's the issue of your grandson, Richard. How can you be sure he will follow the script? It's very important that he does – for confidence in you, in the Pincent Pharma brand. You know that, don't you?'

'Of course I do,' Richard said. 'Trust me, Peter knows what he has to do.' He could feel his blood pressure rising, could feel his heart pounding away in his chest like an out-of-control train rushing down the tracks; he would need a new one in a matter of days, would ensure that one was grown for him immediately.

'I hope so, for your sake,' Hillary said darkly. Richard turned his chair around so that he could look out at the river. Across the river he could see the dim, dull lights of the Authorities' various buildings. All afternoon Pincent Pharma's switchboard had been inundated by calls from people within those same buildings perturbed by the lack of light emanating from his side of the river, asking with barely concealed delight whether there were 'any problems'. He knew full well that there was nothing the Secretary General would like more than an excuse to take Pincent Pharma into state control. Today had to go well. Peter had to follow the script.

'Shall we go?' he asked, forcing a smile.

'Yes,' Hillary said sternly, standing up and brushing out imagined creases in her skirt. 'Let's.'

Mr Samuels pointed to the programmer's vacated chair; when Jude sat down, it was hot and wet from his sweat.

'And now,' Mr Samuels said, 'you will tell me everything you know. If you don't, you will experience pain beyond anything you have ever imagined. Do I make myself clear?'

'Perfectly,' Jude said calmly. He expected to be terrified, was waiting for the panic to set in. But, strangely, he felt neither of those things. He felt alive. He felt, for the first time in his whole life, like he mattered, like he was part of something good.

He pretended to frown at the computer screen. 'You want me to track the problem with your energy? My rate is five thousand a day,' he said.

'Four of my guards are dead,' Mr Samuels said, his voice low and angry. 'Is it a coincidence that guards were killed on the very day you enter the building?

That our energy system goes down also? I don't believe in coincidence, Jude.'

'Dead?' Jude said, shaking his head incredulously and noting archly to himself that Derek Samuels wasn't mentioning anything about some missing Surpluses. 'But you can't think I had anything to do with it. I've been locked up all this time.'

Derek Samuels stared at him icily for a few seconds before standing up. 'You have five minutes,' he said. 'Five minutes to tell me what's going on.'

Jude's eyes flicked down to his watch. The press conference would be starting soon. He was fairly sure Derek Samuels would want to be there.

'Look, I wish I could help, I do,' he said, playing for time. 'But this is really nothing to do with me. None of it.'

As he spoke, the door flew open and a man appeared in the doorway.

'Derek, we're starting now.'

Jude felt his heart quicken as he realised who it was. Richard Pincent, regularly described as the most powerful man in the world. He was wearing a suit; his voice was relaxed. He didn't know, Jude realised. He couldn't know.

'The guards are in place,' Derek Samuels said, immediately standing up. 'I'll be right behind you.'

Richard nodded, then he moved closer, his eyes glistening dangerously. 'Behind me?' he asked. 'No, Derek, not behind me. You'll go now and you'll get Peter. You will escort him personally to the lobby and you will satisfy yourself that everything is as it should be. Then you will make it absolutely clear to my grandson that if he does not do exactly as he is told, his little friend will be locked up for the rest of her short life. Do you understand? There will be no more problems today. Nothing will go wrong – do I make myself absolutely clear?'

'Yes, sir. Perfectly.' Mr Samuels nodded; Jude could see a drop of sweat wending its way down the side of his face. 'Mr Pincent, about the girl.'

'Yes?' His face was like thunder, Jude found himself thinking. 'She's been dealt with?'

Derek Samuels hesistated. 'Yes, sir. Yes, that's right.'

'Good. I'm waiting, Derek.'

'Of course, sir.' Derek Samuels grabbed two guards and ordered them to hold Jude. 'Hold on to him until the conference is over,' he said. 'Keep him where you can see him. Where I can see him. Where everyone can see him,' he said, his own fear appearing to compound his anger. He leant in close so that his face was just centimetres from Jude's. 'Once everyone has gone,' he whispered darkly, 'you and I are going to spend some time together. By the end of it, you'll be begging to tell me everything. And if I let you go, eventually, you'll still never be free. Because you'll always know that I'm there, behind you, watching everything you do, waiting to hurt you again. You can run as far as you like, fabricate as many identities as you like, but you won't escape me. No one ever does.'

Chapter Thirty-three

The Pincent Pharma lobby seemed strangely silent without the constant whirring of the escalators. Rows of chairs were filled with journalists waiting silently; Richard watched them for a second or two before making his way to the front. He had arranged for a spotlight to shine on him as he mounted the podium; it had exactly the effect he'd hoped for. As he walked towards the lectern, the assembled journalists gasped and stared up at him, the prophet on the mount, the bearer of light. Gravely, he looked out over the Pincent Pharma lobby. Every newspaper was represented; every news feed, every radio station.

To the right, Peter sat with Derek Samuels on one side watching him, to keep him in check, and Hillary on the other. In front of Peter were the exact words that he was to say to the journalists. Richard looked over briefly and noticed that Hillary was watching him beadily.

Richard stepped forward.

'Welcome, one and all,' he said confidently, his voice resounding across the lobby. 'Welcome to a most important press conference. And may I apologise wholeheartedly for our energy cut-out this afternoon – we are upgrading our current system and this temporary lapse in power was unfortunately a side effect of the implementation programme. However, as you can see, everything is now back to normal. So, to the point of today's press conference – I'm delighted to have with me Hillary Wright, Deputy Secretary General of the Authorities, and Peter Pincent, my grandson who, as some of you will know, has been working with me over the past few weeks.'

Richard frowned slightly as he noticed two guards whispering fervently to each other, their faces serious; they felt his gaze upon them and immediately fell silent. Richard's eyes narrowed for a moment, then he smiled back at his audience.

'As I think was intimated in your invitations to today's event, there are two significant announcements that we are making today; both are close to my heart and both, I think, will emphasise the continued commitment of the Pincents, and Pincent Pharma, to the Authorities' aims of Comfort, Health, Wealth and Learning. For today we are launching the prototype of Longevity+, the next phase of Longevity, which could be in production in as soon as six months, pending Authorities' approval which, I understand, is very likely to be forthcoming.'

Two doctors appeared at the back of the hall. Richard frowned – they worked in Unit X. He hadn't asked them to attend. But instead of sitting down, they seemed intent on talking to a guard; moments later, they left with two of them.

'Imagine, if you will,' Richard continued, smiling at the journalists before him, his fingers drumming on the lectern, 'feeling as you did when you were truly young. As young as my grandson here, in fact.'

Everyone now stared at Peter. Feeling slightly warm under the lights, Richard took the opportunity to pull out a handkerchief, and he mopped his brow before quickly scanning his notes.

'Imagine feeling that sense of vitality, of energy, every morning,' he continued. His eyes flickered over to Hillary – her face was stony, unreadable. 'Imagine, if you will, the benefits of Longevity being extended to the outer body as well as the inner one. Because that, in a nutshell, is Longevity+. Renewal in the fullest sense of the word. Not just eternal life, but eternal youth.'

The assembled reporters gasped and looked suitably impressed.

'Of course,' Richard said seriously, beginning to relax slightly, 'such drugs are not produced easily. There are funding requirements, extensive research, substantial production costs. But,' he said, turning again to Hillary before beaming at the reporters in front of him, 'I am confident that the Authorities will meet the needs and desires of our people and ensure that funding of Longevity+ is prioritised above all other funding areas.'

He met Hillary's eyes; she smiled thinly.

'Before I ask Hillary to talk to you about grants and funding, perhaps you will allow me to move on to the second announcement of the day – a personal announcement, as it happens, but one which I believe also has a wider significance. For today, my grandson, Peter Pincent, is to sign the Declaration.' He shot a benevolent look in Peter's direction; Peter looked back stonily. 'As you will know, Peter has had a difficult start in life, a chequered past, if you will. But he is a Pincent, something which he has demonstrated all too well in his time at Pincent Pharma. I wanted you all to share in this momentous step for him, his move into adulthood, into this brave and wondrous world that Longevity has created for us. Ladies and gentlemen, my grandson, Peter.'

Unsteadily, Peter rose to his feet. He made his way to the podium, where his grandfather was carefully flattening out his Declaration and motioning for the photographer to make his way over in order to catch the moment. With a flourish, he handed Peter a pen and moved back so that Peter could sign.

'Right there, at the bottom,' he said, under his breath. 'One signature. Do it quickly.'

Peter stared at the document.

'Do it or Anna disappears for ever, you understand?' Richard hissed, then grinned at the photographers surrounding them. 'Stage fright, I think,' he said jovially. 'Boy's not used to all this attention.'

Then, suddenly, Peter looked up at the journalists.

'Actually,' he said seriously, 'I'd like to say a few words. If that's OK?'

Richard felt his chest constrict. 'A few words?' he said through gritted teeth, moving in and trying to manoeuvre Peter away from the podium. 'Peter, perhaps now isn't the time for . . .'

'Speak!' A journalist interrupted. 'Let's hear from Peter Pincent.'

'Yes. Peter Pincent,' another chimed.

Reluctantly, Richard let go of his grandson. 'Very well,' he said, smiling benevolently again, for the benefit of the reporters. 'A few words.' Then he turned around. 'Think of the girl before you say anything stupid,' he whispered into Peter's ear. 'You will be sending her to a place far worse than Grange Hall, and this time there will be no escape. She will die in there, believe me.'

Peter nodded soberly, and moved towards the microphone.

'As my grandfather has said, I've been at Pincent Pharma a while now, and in that time I've learnt a great deal about science, about Longevity, about the beauty of those white pills, the work that has gone into them, the potential they release,' he said. Around him, journalists were nodding and taking notes, and he took a deep breath.

'Each of us, I think, reaches a point where we search for the meaning in life, the point of it all. And my time at Pincent Pharma has really helped me in my search,' he said. 'It's made me realise what's important. Family. Loyalty. Progress.'

He shot a smile at his grandfather, who was staring at him, a false smile fixed on his face.

'Which is why,' he said calmly, 'I am not going to be signing the Declaration today. Or any day, in fact.'

There was a gasp from the floor.

'Of course you are,' his grandfather interrupted menacingly. 'Of course he is. Right now. Aren't you, Peter?'

Peter smiled. 'Actually, no. You see, what I want is life. A real life, full of moments of joy, of anguish, of irritation, of fun. A life with an end point, which makes each second important. A life that is full of love, that doesn't cause suffering and pain. Because that's what Longevity does. It enslaves people, it ruins them.

'This,' he said quickly pulling off his prized ring, the ring he'd kept so carefully. 'I thought it represented life. I thought it was important. But it isn't.' He looked at the ring for a second, the flower engraved on one side, 'AF' engraved on the other. Albert Fern. His great-grandfather's ring. Looking back at the assembled journalists, he hurled it to the back of the room, throwing his grandfather a triumphant look. 'It's a Pincent family heirloom. And I despise the Pincents. I'd rather die than be a Pincent.'

'And who knows, you may get your wish,' his grandfather hissed angrily, as two guards appeared at Peter's side, and started to drag him off the podium.

'I don't want anything to do with this place where Surpluses are tortured, where breeding farms are set up just so that people don't have to have wrinkles. I want a life where people actually enjoy themselves,' Peter shouted. 'A life where people have children and mess and they don't bury their heads in the sand and ignore what's going on around them . . .'

'You will regret this,' his grandfather whispered angrily as he passed him. 'Anna too.'

'You don't even know where Anna is,' Peter shot back. 'You should look for the Surpluses, too, while you're at it.' He tried to push the guards off, but they were too strong for him; a heavy hand clamped over his mouth, silencing him as they dragged him towards the side of the lobby.

His grandfather's face crumpled with confusion; Peter shot him a triumphant parting glance as he was pulled away.

'Wait! Peter! What was that about breeding farms?' a journalist shouted, jumping to his feet.

Another stood up. 'Mr Pincent,' he called out, 'is it true that Surpluses are being tortured to make Longevity+? Do you have anything to say about your grandson's accusations?'

Richard looked around, thinking quickly. Peter was struggling violently with his guards; more and more journalists were standing up, shouting their questions.

'Ladies and gentlemen,' he called out, raising his hands to calm them. 'Ladies and gentlemen, please, a moment.'

The noise level reduced slightly; some of the journalists sat down.

'As you know,' Richard continued, his eyes moving beadily around the room, 'my grandson Peter started out life as a Surplus, brainwashed by the Underground's pernicious members, moulded into a dangerous and criminal mind. His mother was also a criminal, and perhaps that should have been a warning to me. I had hoped very much that by employing him here, by giving him the best chances available, he might be rehabilitated.' He shook his head. 'Sadly, I think that today has shown that reha-bilitation is simply impossible. It is evident to me now that Surpluses are not able to adapt into our civilised society, that they can't grasp the opportunities that we offer them. We want what's best for them, ladies and gentlemen, but that doesn't mean they want what's best for themselves . . .'

'Are you saying that Surpluses shouldn't be made Legal?' a journalist shouted out. 'Are you saying your grandson shouldn't be allowed his freedom?'

'I'm saying,' Richard said levelly, 'that perhaps we need to review the Surplus Act. I'm saying that what Peter has said today is full of lies, full of misin-formation. He knows nothing of the workings of Pincent Pharma, or of the development of Longevity+. I'm saying that I apologise for his outburst. I should have realised how completely the Underground had brainwashed him; should have anticipated that he might try to sabotage this important event.'

There was a murmuring on the floor, a few nods of agreement. Then the murmuring became more vocal as the journalists began to turn to the back of the lobby. Frowning, Richard Pincent noticed someone moving at the back of the room. Then he heard a gasp, more gasps, and someone shouting, 'He's got a gun.' It was only then that he saw the youth. At first he thought that a guard was holding him, then he realised that it was the boy who was pressing something into the guard's back and dragging him to the side of the room.

'Another Surplus,' he said quickly, his voice faltering now, his eyes wide with fear, with shock. 'People, this is a mounting crisis. We must find a way to deal with these criminal youths.'

'You'd like that, wouldn't you?' Jude said angrily, pushing the guard ahead of him and holding the gun out where everyone could see it. 'Only I'm afraid I'm not a Surplus. Nor's Peter. So you can't harvest our cells to make your Longevity drugs. Or is it only girl Surpluses you can use?'

The room hushed; Richard looked at the boy in alarm. 'I'm afraid I have no idea what you're talking about,' he said icily. 'Guards, do something. Restrain this boy.'

'Anyone comes near me and this guard dies,' Jude shouted. 'I work for the Underground. I've got a gun and I'm not afraid to use it.'

'You think I care if you kill a guard? They're ten a

penny,' Richard said angrily, then blanched slightly as he noticed all the guards in the room staring at him, their eyes full of shock and resentment.

'What if I kill you?' Jude said calmly. 'What will you do then? Or what about if I don't kill you? What about if I tell you instead that footage from Unit X is on tape? That I've got evidence of the Surplus girls you've been keeping there? Creating embryos for your precious drugs. Why don't you tell the journalists about that? Why don't you tell them about their screams?'

Richard Pincent went white. 'It's lies,' he said, his voice catching. 'It's all lies.' He stepped back, grabbed Derek Samuels. 'The Surplus girls,' he hissed. 'Where are they? And Anna?'

Derek Samuels didn't need to say anything; his expression, the greeny tinge to his face, said it all. Disgusted, Richard let go of him.

'Lies that will soon be coming to a computer terminal near you,' Jude was saying. 'Unless you let Peter go. Unless you cancel the launch of Longevity+.'

'How dare you!' Richard was white now, struggling to comprehend what the boy was saying, trying to understand what was happening. He was shaking with rage, his eyes bulbous, his hands tightened into fists. 'How dare you threaten me. I am Richard Pincent. I will not have this. I will not . . .' He felt a stabbing pain in his left arm, and looked around wildly. 'I will not have anyone question my methods, question my . . .' But he didn't finish his sentence;

instead, he clutched his chest and fell to the floor.

'He's dead!' a journalist cried out, as two doctors rushed forward. 'The Surpluses have killed him.'

Like sheep, the journalists began to leave their seats, rushing to the front of the room to get a better view. Immediately, Hillary stood up.

'I think,' she said, taking the microphone, 'that we've seen enough. Please return to your seats.'

The journalists didn't move. 'Is it true about Unit X?' one shouted.

'Who's the other boy?' another called out.

'Are you really creating embryos?' another cried. 'Here, at Pincent Pharma?'

As the journalists' questions became louder, more insistent, Hillary looked over at the doctors who were moving Richard on to his side. 'He needs heart regeneration,' one said. 'He's got one waiting.'

Hillary nodded, then she turned to the microphone and held up her hands until a semblance of quiet had been restored. 'Ladies and gentlemen,' she said, her voice crisp and authoritative, 'as Deputy Secretary General, I would like to apologise for today's proceedings. 'As you will appreciate, Pincent Pharma has been encountering some . . . problems recently. May I make it clear that the Authorities take allegations of malpractice and abuse of Surpluses very seriously indeed and that a full inquiry will be launched immediately. I will be taking over the running of Pincent Pharma while Mr Pincent undergoes medical assessment and treatment. In the meantime, and to protect the impartiality of our inquiry, I know that you will understand that there will be no reporting of this press conference or the events surrounding it. Cameras, notebooks and recording devices will, as a matter of national security, be confiscated as you leave.'

'Leave?' a journalist cried out. 'We can't leave. Tell us about the Surpluses.'

'Tell us about Longevity+,' someone else shouted. 'Tell us how it's really made.'

Hillary regarded her audience coolly, then allowed her eyes to rest on the first journalist. 'And your name is?'

The man shifted uncomfortably. 'Tom Wellings.'

'Well, Tom, I'm afraid that you are mistaken. You *will* leave, under Authorities' mandate. Failure to comply with an Authorities' mandate results, as you well know, in arrest and investigation.'

She smiled sweetly at him, then turned to the second journalist. 'And you? Your name, please?'

'Sarah,' the woman said, her voice firm. 'Sarah Condon.'

'Well, Ms Condon, when the inquiry results are published – which they will be, because the Authorities are committed to total transparency – you will be able to report them accurately for your readers. I would hate for any of you to face sedition charges before you're able to do that. Really I would.'

She stared at the woman, who, looking shaken, sat down again.

'I do regret the inconvenience,' Hillary continued. 'However, your loyalty and support will be recognised with an exclusive from the Authorities on the Energy Forum tomorrow. And to show our gratitude, each of you will receive ten extra energy coupons next month, assuming, of course, that no details of today's events have made their way into the public arena. Thank you, and please do make your way out of the building now.'

No one moved for a few seconds, then, gradually, as the guards began to move through the room, the journalists began to stand up. One by one, their belongings were taken from them and they were ushered out of the building into the night. A stretcher appeared; Richard Pincent was lifted on to it. Derek Samuels followed the guards carrying it.

Eventually the room was empty, but for Jude, who was still holding his gun, the guard he was training it on, and Peter and the guards holding him. Hillary waved away Peter's guards; Jude watched carefully as they left the building, then sent the guard he'd been holding after them, holding the gun at his side, just in case. Hillary turned to him, her lips pursed. 'These tapes,' she said, her voice brittle. 'You will give me all copies, do you understand?'

Jude looked at her in disgust. 'So you can destroy them?'

'So that we can investigate your claims fully,' Hillary said silkily.

'File them away, you mean.'

Hillary smiled. 'The Authorities will follow due procedure,' she said. 'And I'm afraid you don't have a choice. Either you give me the tapes, or I'll have you arrested, do I make myself clear?'

Jude looked at her for a moment, then reached into his pocket and handed over a disk. Hillary took it, her eyes lighting up. 'And now you will give me the gun,' she said icily. 'You won't get out of here alive unless you do.'

But Jude just laughed. 'You really think there's only one copy?' he asked. 'You really think I'm that stupid?'

Hillary hesitated. 'More copies?'

'Of course there are,' Peter said, taking his lead from Jude. 'The Surpluses have been rescued. Anna's safe. And believe me there are more copies of the disk. The images have been transmitted into cyberspace. Anything happens to us and they will be everywhere.'

Hillary's eyes narrowed. She turned back to Jude who had one eyebrow raised.

'He's right,' he shrugged. 'If you don't let us go, things could be very bad for you.'

'For Richard Pincent, you mean,' Hillary corrected him. 'He is at fault here, not the Authorities.'

'Right,' Peter said, sarcastically. 'And the fact that you knew all about it isn't important? What was it you said . . . "Who'd have thought Surpluses could be so useful?" You think that will go down well in the inquiry?'

Hillary's eyes widened in shock.

'See? It's not just the Surpluses we've got on tape,' Peter said levelly. 'Let us go, or it goes public.'

Hillary was silent for a few moments, then she took a deep breath. 'I want you to go,' she said, her voice angry and low. 'I want you to go, and I want you to disappear. Breathe one word about what happened here today, raise your heads above the parapet just slightly, and you'll know the power and ruthlessness of the Authorities, do I make myself clear?'

'Sure, whatever,' Jude said, turning to leave.

Peter, meanwhile, was still staring at Hillary. 'And you come near me or my family and you'll know the power and ruthlessness of the Underground,' he said bitterly. 'Do *I* make *myself* clear?' He moved over quickly to stand beside Jude. Then, slowly, surely, they walked towards the door, looking over their shoulders as they did so, then down the steps, and through the gates. A man emerged from the trees outside the compound, giving the sign of the Underground, and they followed him in silence to the main road, then through a deserted builders' yard to a road on the other side where a car was waiting for them.

'You know the disk I gave her was a list of codes from one of my clients,' Jude said, as they approached the car.

Peter frowned at him, then smiled wryly. 'So you don't have anything on tape?' he asked.

'Not a thing,' Jude winked. 'But she doesn't know that. Not yet, anyway.'

Quickly, they got into the car and it sped off, down back roads, on to a dual carriageway, into the country. Every so often Peter turned round, his darting eyes checking for other cars on the road, for any sign of danger.

'I guess we're going to be doing a lot of that in the future. Looking over our shoulders, I mean,' Jude said thoughtfully.

'Welcome to my life,' Peter said with a shrug. Then he looked at Jude and grinned. 'Actually, I mean it. Welcome to my life.'

Chapter Thirty-four

Peter stared at the computer screen uncertainly as it flickered into life. Tentatively, he moved his hands towards the keyboard which was wedged on the kitchen counter, between two boxes of cereal and the solar-powered toaster, and started to type.

> *Peter2124: Jude are you there? Don't know if this is going to work. Let me know if gets through. Peter.*

He only had to wait a few seconds for a reply.

> *Jude2124: Loud and clear.*
>
> *Peter2124: So how's things?*
>
> *Jude2124: Things? I couldn't possibly tell you about any things; Pip would have to kill me. And then you.*

Peter chuckled, imagining Jude's impatience with Pip's demands, imagining them bickering as they had bickered in the few days they'd shared together after escaping from Pincent Pharma. To Peter it had been like old times – hiding in cellars, making plans to leave London – but infinitely better because this time he hadn't felt alone. He'd had Anna, he'd had Ben, and he'd had Jude. Jude, who made everyone laugh, who rolled his eyes at everything, who thought he knew better than everyone, who reminded Peter of himself more than he ever cared to admit.

Peter2124: Is he still fixated on the weather for passwords?

Jude2124: He's moved on to flora and fauna. I tried to get him to use something else, but he wasn't having any of it. Did you get the package I sent, by the way?

Peter looked down at the small box on the floor beside him. It had arrived that morning. In it, to his surprise, to his relief, he'd found his ring, the one he'd thrown away, the one he didn't want but which his hand felt naked without.

Peter2124: Where did you get it? I don't want it. I threw it away, remember?

Jude2124: Of course I remember. It hit the guard holding me when you threw it away at the end of your little speech at Pincent Pharma. Gave me an opportunity to get out the gun Pip gave me. I think maybe it's a lucky ring.

Peter frowned.

Peter2124: So you kept it for a few weeks, then. What were you going to do, sell it?

Jude2124: Wish I had now, since you're so sure you don't want it. Probably worth a bit.

Peter bit his lip.

Jude2124: Actually, I kind of liked it. Thought I'd wear it. But it's yours. Pip said you should hold on to it.

Peter2124: The AF. It stands for Albert Fern.

Jude2124: That's what Pip said. He's the guy who invented Longevity, right? You. certainly have some interesting relatives, don't you.

Peter2124: Interesting's one word for it. Fine, I'll keep the ring. Thanks for looking after it for me.

Jude2124: You're welcome. So you're happy out there, wherever it is you are?

Peter looked out of the window, over the fields stretching out into the distance.

Peter2124: Really happy, yeah.

As he typed the words, he found himself smiling – he actually was happy, he realised. Properly happy, probably for the first time ever. They'd been here for a few weeks now; their location secret, chosen for its remoteness, its seclusion. The Authorities would be looking for them but for now, at least, they were safe; safe and free at last. He and Anna had land, were determined to be self-sufficient, and for the first time in his life Peter felt in control, unburdened. Ben had started to walk and say the odd word, and their unborn child had begun to move inside Anna, making its presence felt with fluttering movements and forcing Peter to work as hard as he could to feed the insatiable hunger it had created in its mother. It had already enslaved him, he realised, just as he'd been warned it would, just as the land he now worked and nature herself enslaved him with constant demands, with rain, with wind, with dark nights and bright mornings. What he hadn't known was that he'd be enslaved willingly; that he would meet the whims of his taskmasters with love, with devotion, with joy in his heart.

Jude2124: And there's really no one there? You're living in the wilderness? Can't think of anything worse myself.

Peter grinned. Their nearest neighbour was over five miles away – even in over-populated Britain, the wilds of northern Scotland still provided solitude.

Peter2124: You kind of get a taste for it. So how about you? How's Sheila?

Jude2124: Sheila? She's fine. So far she's failed to fall for my many charms, but she'll succumb eventually. She certainly talks a lot. Says I've been badly trained. Says I wouldn't have lasted a minute in Grange Hall.

Peter grinned.

Peter2124: To be honest, I think she's right.

Jude2124: So look, I'd better go. Can't risk anyone tracking you now, can we? You're sure you've got your security codes set up properly?

Peter2124: I think so.

Jude2124: I'll take a look later to be safe. I'll let you know if you've got any vulnerabilities. Pip says to remember there's a doctor ready to fly up the minute you need it. He says good luck with everything.

Peter2124: Thanks. I think I'm going to need it.

He thought of them, all of them, back in London

somewhere, wherever the latest Underground head-quarters was, planning, waiting, hiding. And he knew that he would return, that soon he'd be with them again, but for now he was grateful to be far away, to be at peace, even if he knew it was a chimera, impermanent. He was about to close down his computer, when another message flashed on the screen suddenly.

Jude2124: I take it you heard about your grandfather.

Peter felt his jaw tighten. He had heard – the inquiry had found Richard Pincent negligent, but not criminally liable. He was back at Pincent Pharma; his only punishment had been to complete a ReTraining programme in health and safety.

Peter2124: I heard, yes. What about Unit X? Has it been shut down?

Jude2124: Apparently. They said they're working on a synthetic alternative. But Pip says it's only a sop. He says people are asking questions, though, and that's the important thing. Didn't stop the Authorities sending me my Declaration, of course. Like I'm going to do anything but burn the thing.

Peter nodded thoughtfully. He heard a noise behind him and turned to see Anna wandering in, a pail of water in her right hand and Ben clutching her left. She gave him a kiss as she passed him, and he grabbed her quickly, ignoring her cries of protest as the water spilled and Ben immediately ran to jump in it.

His face breaking out involuntarily into a smile,

Peter turned back to his computer.

Peter2124: Say hi to Pip and Sheila.

Jude2124. I will. See you, then. Over and out. PS
Click this.

Curiously, Peter clicked the link; seconds later, an image filled his screen: it showed several men attacking a Pincent Pharma truck, destroying its contents; one of the men stuck his fingers up at the camera filming him – his face was covered by a balaclava, but Peter knew who it was.

'Is that who I think it is?' Anna asked, peering over to look.

'Sure is,' Peter nodded. Then he kissed Anna's hand and, grinning to himself, made his way out to the yard.

About the author

Gemma Malley studied Philosophy at Reading University before working as a journalist. She edited several business magazines and contributed regularly to *Company Magazine* and the *Sunday Telegraph* before moving into the civil service in a senior communications role at Ofsted. *The Declaration*, her first novel for a teenage audience, was published to critical acclaim. *The Resistance* is the sequel and *The Revelation*, to be published in September 2010, will complete the trilogy. She lives in South London with her family.

Every journey has a first step.

Every story has a beginning.

Experience Anna and Peter's
from the very start . . .

'Should be on everyone's reading list because it has you clinging on for dear life around every twist and turn' *Sunday Express*